D1832935

MAHA-BHARATA

MAHA-BHARATA

THE EPIC OF ANCIENT INDIA

ROMESH DUTT, C. I. E.

WITH AN INTRODUCTION BY
THE RIGHT HON. F. MAX MULLER

GYAN

Published by

GYAN

Gyan Publishing House
5, Ansari Road
Daryaganj, New Delhi-110002
Phone: 011-47034999, 9811692060
E-mail: books@gyanbooks.com

Distribution Network
gyanbooks.com
India, USA, Canada, UK, Australia, France

© Publisher

All rights reserved. No part of this work may be reproduced, stored, adapted, or transmitted in any form or by any means, electronic, mechanical, photocopying, micro-filming, recording or otherwise, or translated in any language, without the prior written permission of the copyright owner and the publisher.

ISBN: 978-81-212-8646-6 (PB)
First Published, 1898

2nd Impression 2023

Printed at: Gyan Press, Delhi.

The book is sold subject to the condition that it shall not, by way of trade or otherwise, be lent, resold, hired out, or otherwise circulated without the prior publisher's written consent.

MAHA-BHARATA
Author: ROMESH DUTT

MAHA-BHARATA

वनगमनम्।

The Banishment

MAHA-BHARATA

The EPIC *of* ANCIENT INDIA CONDENSED *into* ENGLISH VERSE

By ROMESH DUTT, C.I.E.

WITH AN INTRODUCTION BY
THE RIGHT HON. F. MAX MÜLLER

TWELVE PHOTOGRAVURES FROM
ORIGINAL ILLUSTRATIONS
DESIGNED FROM INDIAN
SOURCES BY E. STUART
HARDY

LONDON
J. M. DENT & CO.
29 & 30 BEDFORD STREET, W.C.
MDCCCXCIX

INTRODUCTION

WE possess but very little of true Epic Poetry, and the wonder is that we should possess any. Of course if we define an epic as a poem which in the form of continuous narrative celebrates the achievements of one or more heroic personages of history or tradition, any poet may write an epos. But if by epos are meant early unwritten narrative poems celebrating incidents of heroic tradition, we can easily understand why their number should be so small as it is. Strictly speaking, I know of one true epic poem only, the Kalewala of the Fins, and possibly the Kalewipoeg of the Estonians. These were preserved to the present day, and are still living in the mouths of the people. They were never written down till they were lately collected and fitted together, without any additions, by such men as Von Becker, Lönnrot, Castrén, and others. Lönnrot's first edition of the Kalewala in Finnish appeared in 1835, comprising about 12,000 verses in thirty-two songs. This was translated into Swedish by Castrén in 1841. In 1849, however, Lönnrot published a new edition, consisting of 22,793 verses in fifty songs, and a German translation by Schiefner appeared in 1857. More songs even, all forming integral parts of a large epic poem, have been discovered since the death of Castrén and Lönnrot. While we may perfectly trust the painstaking scholarship and conscientious accuracy of Castrén, Lönnrot, and other Finnish students in their treatment of these ancient popular poems of Finland, some doubt has been thrown on the perfect authenticity of the Estonian poems of Kalewipoeg as collected by Kreutzwald and translated into German by Reinthal, 1857. They were found to be in a much more fragmentary state, and it is supposed that they were largely restored, while in the case of the Kalewala we possess the trustworthy copy of poems exactly as they were, and are still recited in Finland by old men and women in the presence of their Swedish auditors.

All other epic poems, after existing for an unknown length of time in the tradition of popular poets, have passed through what is called a *Diaskeué*, a setting in order, a dressing or recension at the hands of later poets. The most perfect specimen of this kind of epic poetry exists in the two Homeric poems, the Iliad and Odyssey. How the component parts of these poems, such as the Cyclopeia, the story of the wooden horse at Troy, the Nekyia, the Doloneia, the Patrokleia, &c., had existed before they formed part of an Odyssey and Iliad, we can see in the case of Demodokos and other Aoidoi who sang these Aristeias at festivals, both public and private. But we have no trustworthy information as to how these poems came to be collected, whether their dialect and metre were changed in the schools of the Homeridæ, and at what time the first written copies of them were prepared and circulated. I doubt whether in Greece the very idea of a written literature existed much before 500 or 600 B.C., that is, before the first contact between West and East. There is the Greek alphabet, which tells us in the clearest way that the Greeks learnt their letters from the Phœnicians; but there is a long distance between a knowledge of the A B C and its employment for inscriptions, coins, and even for official treaties, and its use for literary purposes. I confess that the well-known passage at the end of the Phædrus gives me the impression as if even Plato had still a recollection of the time when literature was mnemonic only, and not yet written.

And if we look at the epic literature of other nations, we find much the same. The poem of the Nibelunge, such as we possess it, was composed and written down about A.D. 1200; but we see from the short ballads recording the fates of Sigurd and Brynhild, as preserved to us in the Edda, what the poems may have been like which were used as his materials by the unknown German Homer of the twelfth century.

Firdusi, the author of the Persian national epic, the Shâh Nâmeh, Book of Kings, about A.D. 1000, tells us himself what sources he consulted, and how he travelled about from village to village to collect the materials for his great poem.

We see, therefore, that the constituent elements of the epic poems which we possess—the Iliad, the Odyssey, the Nibelunge, and the Shâh Nâmeh—existed in oral tradition long before the invention of writing; that they were elaborated during what is called the Mnemonic Period of literature; and that they were reduced to their present form at a time when the art of alphabetic writing had been discovered, and had been applied, not only to inscriptions, but to poetry and other literary compositions; when, in fact, there were not only a few sculptors to engrave official documents, but a large public that could both read and write.

We must distinguish, therefore, between two kinds of epic poetry—one, the *Mnemonic*, as preserved intact in the Kalewala, and slightly recast in the Kalewipoeg; another, the *Literary*, which has passed through the hands of later poets, such as Iliad and Odyssey, the Nibelungenlied, and the Shâh Nâmeh. There is a third class of purely *Artificial* epic poems, written in imitation of these models, such as Virgil's Æneid, Wolfram von Eschenbach's Parzival, the Lusiads of Camoens, and, lastly, poems like Voltaire's Henriade. But these belong to quite a different sphere of poetry.

It is not likely that the number of true epic poems will ever be increased, and the discovery of two epic poems in India was therefore a great event in the comparative study of ancient literature. These two Sanskrit poems were the Mahâbhârata and the Râmâya*n*a. Leaving here out of consideration the Râmâya*n*a, the author of which, Valmîki, seems to have been more than a mere Diaskeuastes, we have the Mahâbhârata, an ancient Sanskrit poem, which, in its present form, is said to consist of no less than 90,000 couplets, and was published at Calcutta in 1834–39 in four large quarto volumes. In its present form it can hardly be called a poem. It is an enormous poetical treasury, in which everything was thrown that could possibly be brought into connection with its original story. At first the Mahâbhârata was the story of the Great War that had been waged in ancient times in India, but after the popular songs about that "Eighteen Days' War" had been collected, not only ancient stories, but ancient laws, customs, and philosophies were all incorporated into it. The date of its first composition is, of course, unknown, as much as the age of the single Aristeias of Iliad and Odyssey, or of the various Kvidhas of the Edda. All we can say is, that a collected poem, called not only Bhârata, but Mahâbhârata, *i.e.* the great story of the war of the Bhâratas, is mentioned clearly in the Â*s*valâyana Sûtras, that is, before the rise of Buddhism in the sixth century B.C. But what the Mahâbhârata was then, we shall of course never know. All we can say is that, when first collected, it must have been a mnemonic poem, composed before the art of writing was known in India, or, at all events, before it had been applied to literary purposes in that country. Extraordinary as it may seem to us that so enormous a poem should have been composed and handed down by memory only, the fact itself can hardly be doubted. It is in India, of all countries in the world, where we must study the facts about the extraordinary, and to us almost incredible, powers of memory, before the art of writing was known and practised. There is, no doubt, an introductory chapter of our poem which tells us how, with the help of Ganesa, the Mahâbhârata was written. But the absence of that chapter in a large number of MSS., more particularly, as Dr. Winternitz has shown, in the MSS. of the south of India, speaks for itself, and proves that the idea of the poem having been composed on paper was an afterthought, and may, in fact, serve to determine the time when writing for literary purposes became the custom in India. The poet is called Vyâsa, or Krishna Dvaipâyana, a name which means "arranger," from *vi* and *as*, to distribute, to extend; and whatever his date may have been, we may be certain that his work, the Mahâbhârata, was a genuine product of the Mnemonic Period of Indian literature.

Life seems too short to read such a gigantic poem as a whole, and various attempts have been made from time to time to reduce it to its original dimensions. The most promising was to follow the indications of an old Index or Anukramanikâ, incorporated in the poem itself. But if we add the number of couplets of each book, as stated in that preface, we are still left with a poem of no less than 85,000 couplets. It is impossible to enjoy such a poem, however beautiful it may be in some of its stories; nor can we imagine that the original poet, or the original collector even, contemplated such a monstrous production. The original subject was the war between two branches of the same royal family, the Bhârata princes. These Bhâratas are mentioned as an ancient and most powerful race in the north of India as early as the Brâhmana period, for in the Satapathabrâhmana, xiii. 5, 4, we read, "The greatness of the Bhâratas neither the men before nor those after them have ever attained; nor did the seven tribes of men, even as mortal man does not touch the sky with his flanks."

It is easy to see how round the nucleus of this war an immense mass of poetry, both popular and artificial, was accumulated, but it was not so easy a task to sift this enormous mass, and to extract from it what may have been the original story. This task has been boldly undertaken and carried through, as far as I can judge, with great success by Mr. Romesh Dutt in his "Mahâbhârata condensed into English Verse." He has himself given an account of the principles by which he was guided in his work. He has, as much as possible, taken a number of verses of the original and rendered them faithfully into English. He has left out on the very largest scale, but he has not added; and the impression which his bold undertaking leaves on the reader is certainly that something like what we here read in English may have been recited in India when the war between the Kurus and the sons of Pâ*nd*u was first sung by the ancient bards of the country. If Vyâsa, the collector, was in any sense the author of some parts of the poem, it is important to observe that in the poem itself he is represented as the kinsman, though under peculiar circumstances, of the royal family of the Bhâratas.

Mr. Romesh Dutt tells us that without exaggeration two hundred millions of Hindus cherish to the present day the story of their ancient epics. "The Hindu," he writes, "scarcely lives, man or woman, high or low, educated or ignorant, whose earliest recollections do not cling round the story and the characters of the Mahâbhârata," listening to it either in the original, or to a translation into one of the many vernaculars. Considering how many people there are now in India who know English better than Sanskrit, there can be little doubt that this English translation and condensation by Mr. Romesh Dutt will be most welcome to his own compatriots. It will be equally welcome to many English students of literature who wish to gain an idea of that wonderful epic. The original, in its colossal bulk, can be consulted by Sanskrit scholars only. It is true it has been translated from beginning to end into English by my late friend Protap Chandra Roy and his assistants, but even that translation will hardly meet with many patient readers in England. To the student of Sanskrit literature the Mahâbhârata, so far as it reflects the ancient life of India, will always remain an invaluable treasury. Quite apart from the story of the ancient heroic war, the great bulk of the later accretions also is full of interest and instruction. Of course there exists always one great difficulty; we cannot tell which period of Indian history is represented to us in each of its various component parts. Every race in the north, the south, the east, and west of India wished to see some account of its own heroes inserted in the national epic. Philosophers claimed some mention of their doctrines as a proof of their antiquity, and as a kind of brief of nobility. Moral and legal authorities clamoured naturally for the same mention; and even mere customs, rules about caste, marriage, and inheritance had to be placed under the shield of the ancient epic. The geography, the ethnology, the migrations of races in India, all may be studied in the Mahâbhârata. The dominating religious cult, not at the time of the Great War itself, but at the time of the final redaction of the poem, was clearly the worship of K*ri*sh*n*a, and this is generally referred to a time after the disappearance of Buddhism from the soil of India, so that the final redaction of the epic can hardly be placed before the Renaissance period of Indian literature, that is, before the fourth century A.D. But much of this is still uncertain, and we must carefully guard against premature and positive assertions when we treat of the chronology of Indian literature, and of its epic literature in particular. Every generation of scholars builds up its own system of chronology, and the next generation pulls it down again. Unfortunately there are no ancient temples, or palaces, or works of art in India to serve as guides. The very idea of stone buildings does not go back beyond the time of the invasion of India by Alexander. The most ancient stone buildings are the buildings dating from Asoka's time in the third century, and though many of them contain relics in the shape of jewels and gold ornaments, they have not yielded as yet any real works of art, not even weapons, or armour, or warlike ornaments. The Mahâbhârata tells us of weapons, which remind us of some of the weapons found by Schliemann at Mycenæ. We find descriptions of golden bosses on the wood of a bow, tipped with gold at either end, and of golden insects worked on the staff of another bow. We read of brilliant suns on other weapons, and of golden fireflies glinting in the yellow light of day. A sword is called toad-engraven, and all these things seem to testify to an early cultivation of arts and crafts of which no remnants have survived. Again, we read of mimes and actors, and of bards reciting ancient songs; but of the poems themselves which they recited, or of the plays which they acted, nothing remains to us, not even their names and titles.

As a mine of information the Mahâbhârata is inexhaustible, and will for a long time remain unexhausted. We are all the more grateful to Mr. Romesh Dutt for having given us a kind of photographic representation, a snap-shot, as it were, of the old poem—the longest poem, I believe, in the whole world—and having enabled students of literature to form for themselves some kind of idea of what our Aryan brothers in India admired and still admire in the epic poetry of their country.

F. MAX MÜLLER.

OXFORD, *January* 1899.

TO

THE MARQUIS OF RIPON

EVER GRATEFULLY REMEMBERED BY MY COUNTRYMEN FOR HIS JUST AND BENEVOLENT ADMINISTRATION AND FOR HIS GENEROUS AND HELPFUL MEASURES FOR THE INTRODUCTION OF SELF-GOVERNMENT IN INDIA

THIS TRANSLATION

OF THE ANCIENT EPIC OF MY COUNTRY IS RESPECTFULLY DEDICATED

A

CONTENTS

LIST OF ILLUSTRATIONS

THE
EPIC OF ANCIENT INDIA

BOOK I

ASTRA DARSANA

(*The Tournament*)

THE scene of the Epic is the ancient kingdom of the Kurus which flourished along the upper course of the Ganges; and the historical fact on which the Epic is based is a great war which took place between the Kurus and a neighbouring tribe, the Panchalas, in the thirteenth or fourteenth century before Christ.

According to the Epic, Pandu and Dhrita-rashtra, who was born blind, were brothers. Pandu died early, and Dhrita-rashtra became king of the Kurus, and brought up the five sons of Pandu along with his hundred sons.

Yudhishthir, the eldest son of Pandu, was a man of truth and piety; Bhima, the second, was a stalwart fighter; and Arjun, the third son, distinguished himself above all the other princes in arms. The two youngest brothers, Nakula and Sahadeva, were twins. Duryodhan was the eldest son of Dhrita-rashtra and was jealous of his cousins, the sons of Pandu. A tournament was held, and in the course of the day a warrior named Karna, of unknown origin, appeared on the scene and proved himself a worthy rival of Arjun. The rivalry between Arjun and Karna is the leading thought of the Epic, as the rivalry between Achilles and Hector is the leading thought of the Iliad.

It is only necessary to add that the sons of Pandu as well as Karna were, like the heroes of Homer, god-born chiefs. Some god inspired the birth of each. Yudhishthir was the son of Dharma or Virtue, Bhima of Vayu or Wind, Arjun of Indra or Rain-god, the twin youngest were the sons of the Aswin twins, and Karna was the son of Surya the Sun, but was believed by himself and by all others to be the son of a simple chariot-driver.

The portion translated in this Book forms Sections cxxxiv. to cxxxvii. of Book i. of the original Epic in Sanscrit (Calcutta edition of 1834).

I

The Gathering

Wrathful sons of Dhrita-rashtra, born of Kuru's royal race!
Righteous sons of noble Pandu, god-born men of godlike grace!

Skill in arms attained these princes from a Brahman warrior bold,
Drona, priest and proud preceptor, peerless chief of days of old!

Out spake Drona to the monarch in Hastina's royal hall,
Spake to Bhishma and to Kripa, spake to lords and courtiers all:

"Mark the gallant princes, monarch, trained in arms and warlike art,
Let them prove their skill and valour, rein the steed and throw the dart!"

Answered then the ancient monarch, joyful was his royal heart,
"Best of Brahmans and of warriors, nobly hast thou done thy part!

Name the place and fix the moment, hold a royal tournament,
Publish wide the laws of combat, and command thy king's consent.

Sightless roll these orbs of vision, dark to me is noonday light,
Happier men will mark the tourney and the peerless princes' fight.

Let the good and wise Vidura serve thy mandate and behest,
Let a father's pride and gladness fill this old and cheerless breast."

Then the good and wise Vidura went unto his duties bound,
Drona, blessed with skill and wisdom, measured out the tourney ground,

Clear of jungle was the meadow, by a crystal fountain graced,
Drona on the lighted altar holy gifts and offerings placed,

Holy was the star auspicious, and the hour was calm and bright,
Men from distant town and hamlet came to view the sacred rite.

Then arose white stately mansions, built by architects of fame,
Decked with arms for Kuru's monarch and for every royal dame,

And the people built their stages circling round the listed green,
And the nobles with their white tents graced the fair and festive scene.

Brightly dawned the festal morning, and the monarch left his hall,
Bhishma and the pious Kripa with the lords and courtiers all,

And they came unto the mansions, gay and glittering, gold-encased,
Decked with gems and rich *baidurya*, and with strings of pearls be-laced.

Fair Gandhari, queen of Kuru, Pritha, Pandu's widowed dame,
Ladies in their gorgeous garments, maids of beauty and of fame,

Mounted to their glittering mansions where the tints harmonious blend,
As, on Meru's golden mountain, queens of heavenly gods ascend!

And the people of the city, Brahmans, Vaisyas, Kshatras bold,
Men from stall and loom and anvil gathered there, the young and old,

And arose the sound of trumpet and the surging people's cry,
Like the voice of angry ocean, tempest-lashed, sublime and high!

Came the saintly white-robed Drona, white his sacrificial thread,
White his sandal-mark and garlands, white the locks that crowned his head,

With his son renowned for valour walked forth Drona, radiant, high,
So the Moon with Mars conjoinéd walks upon the cloudless sky!

Offerings to the gods immortal then the priestly warrior made,
Brahmans with their chanted *mantra* worship and obeisance paid,

And the festive note of *sankha* mingled with the trumpet's sound,
Throngs of warriors, various-armèd, came unto the listed ground.

II

The Princes

Gauntleted and jewel-girdled, now the warlike princes came,
With their stately bows and quivers and their swords like wreaths of flame,

Each behind his elder stepping, good Yudhishthir first of all,
Each his wondrous skill displaying held the silent crowds in thrall,

And the men in admiration marked them with a joyful eye,
Or by sudden panic stricken stooped to let the arrow fly!

Mounted on their rapid coursers oft the princes proved their aim,
Racing, hit the targe with arrows lettered with their royal name,

With their glinting sunlit weapons shone the youths sublime and high,
More than mortals seemed the princes, like *gandharvas* of the sky!

Shouts of joy the people uttered as by sudden impulse driven,
Mingled voice of tens of thousands struck the pealing vault of heaven!

Still the princes shook their weapons, drove the deep resounding car,
Or on steed or tusker mounted waged the glorious mimic war!

Mighty sword and ample buckler, ponderous mace the princes wield,
Brightly gleam their lightning rapiers as they range the listed field,

Brave and fearless is their action, and their movements quick and light,
Skilled and true the thrust and parry of their weapons flaming bright!

III

Bhima and Duryodhan

Bhima came and proud Duryodhan with their maces held on high,
Like two cliffs with lofty turrets cleaving through the azure sky!

In their warlike arms accoutred with their girded loins they stood,
Like two untamed jungle tuskers in the deep and echoing wood!

And as tuskers range the forest, so they range the spacious field,
Right to left and back they wander and their ponderous maces wield!

Unto Kuru's sightless monarch wise Vidura drew the scene,
Pritha proudly of the princes spake unto the Kuru queen.

While the stalwart Bhima battled with Duryodhan brave and strong,
Fierce in wrath, for one or other, shóuted forth the maddened throng,

"Hail to Kuru prince Duryodhan!" "Hail to Bhima hero proud!"
Sounds like these from surging myriads rose in tumult deep and loud.

And with troubled vision Drona marked the heaving restless plain,
Marked the crowd by anger shaken, like the tempest-shaken main,

To his son then whispered Drona quick the tumult to appease,
Part the armed and angry wrestlers, bid the deadly combat cease,

With their lifted clubs the princes slow retire on signal given,
Like the parting of the billows, mighty-heaving, tempest-driven!

Came forth then the ancient Drona on the open battle-ground,
Stopped the drum and lofty trumpet, spake in voice like thunder's
sound:

"Bid him come, the gallant Arjun! pious prince and warrior skilled,
Arjun, born of mighty INDRA, and with VUSHNU's prowess filled."

IV

The Advent of Arjun

Gauntleted and jewel-girdled, with his bow of ample height,
Archer Arjun pious-hearted to the gods performed a rite,

Then he stepped forth proud and stately in his golden mail encased,
Like the sunlit cloud of evening with the golden rainbow graced!

And a gladness stirred the people all around the listed plain,
Voice of drum and blare of trumpet rose with *sankha's* festive strain!

"Mark! the gallant son of Pandu, whom the happy Pritha bore,
Mark! the heir of INDRA's valour, matchless in his arms and lore,

Mark! the warrior young and valiant, peerless in his skill of arms,
Mark! the pure-souled, pious chieftain, decked with grace and varied
charms!"

Pritha heard such grateful voices borne aloft unto the sky,
Milk of love suffused her bosom, tear of joy was in her eye!

And where rested Kuru's monarch, joyous accents struck his ear,
And he turned to wise Vidura seeking for the cause to hear:

"Wherefore like the voice of ocean, when the tempest winds prevail,
Rise these voices of the people and the spacious skies assail?"

Answered him the wise Vidura, "It is Pritha's gallant boy,
Godlike moves in golden armour, and the people shout for joy!"

"Pleased am I," so spake the monarch, "and I bless my happy fate,
Pritha's sons like fires of *yajna* sanctify this mighty State!"

Now the voices of the people died away and all was still,
Arjun to his proud preceptor showed his might and matchless skill,

Towering high or lowly bending, on the turf or on his car,
With his bow and glist'ning arrows Arjun waged the mimic war,

Targets on the wide arena, mighty tough or wondrous small,
With his arrows bright, unfailing, Arjun pierced them one and all!

Wild-boar shaped of solid iron coursed the wide-extending field,
In its jaws five glist'ning arrows sent the archer wondrous-skilled,

Cow-horn by a thread suspended, and by winds unceasing swayed,
One and twenty well-aimed arrows on this moving mark he laid,

And with equal skill his rapier did the godlike Arjun wield,
Whirling round his mace of battle ranged the spacious tourney field!

V

The Advent of Karna

Now the feats of arms are ended, and the closing hour draws nigh,
Music's voice is hushed in silence, and dispersing crowds pass by,

Hark! Like welkin-shaking thunder wakes a deep and deadly sound,
Clank and din of warlike weapons burst upon the tented ground!

Are the solid mountains splitting, is it bursting of the earth,
Is it tempest's pealing accent whence the lightning takes its birth?

Thoughts like these alarm the people for the sound is dread and high,
To the gate of the arena turns the crowd with anxious eye!

Gathered round preceptor Drona, Pandu's sons in armour bright,
Like the five-starred constellation round the radiant Queen of Night,

Gathered round the proud Duryodhan, dreaded for his exploits done,
All his brave and warlike brothers and preceptor Drona's son,

So the gods encircled Indra, thunder-wielding, fierce and bold,
When he scattered Danu's children in the misty days of old!

Pale, before the unknown warrior, gathered nations part in twain,
Conqueror of hostile cities, lofty Karna treads the plain!

In his golden mail accoutred and his rings of yellow gold,
Like a moving cliff in stature, armèd comes the chieftain bold!

Pritha, yet unwedded, bore him, peerless archer on the earth,
Portion of the solar radiance, for the Sun inspired his birth!

Like a tusker in his fury, like a lion in his ire,
Like the sun in noontide radiance, like the all-consuming fire!

Lion-like in build and muscle, stately as a golden palm,
Blessed with every manly virtue, peerless warrior proud and calm!

With his looks serene and lofty field of war the chief surveyed,
Scarce to Kripa or to Drona honour and obeisance made!

Still the panic-stricken people viewed him with unmoving gaze,
Who may be this unknown warrior, question they in hushed amaze!

Then in voice of pealing thunder spake fair Pritha's eldest son,
Unto Arjun, Pritha's youngest, each, alas! to each unknown!

"All thy feats of weapons, Arjun, done with vain and needless boast,
These and greater I accomplish—witness be this mighty host!"

Thus spake proud and peerless Karna in his accents deep and loud,
And as moved by sudden impulse leaped in joy the listening crowd!

And a gleam of mighty transport glows in proud Duryodhan's heart,
Flames of wrath and jealous anger from the eyes of Arjun start!

Drona gave the word, and Karna, Pritha's war-beloving son,
With his sword and with his arrows did the feats by Arjun done!

VI

The Rival Warriors

Joyful was the proud Duryodhan, gladness gleamed upon his face,
And he spake to gallant Karna with a dear and fond embrace:

"Welcome, mighty armḗd chieftain! thou hast victor's honours won!
Thine is all my wealth and kingdom, name thy wish and it is done!"

Answered Karna to Duryodhan, "Prince! thy word is good as deed,
But I seek to combat Arjun and to win the victor's meed!"

"Noble is the boon thou seekest," answered Kuru's prince of fame,
"Be a joy unto your comrades, let the foeman dread thy name!"

Anger flamed in Arjun's bosom, and he spake in accents rude
Unto Karna who in triumph calm and proud and fearless stood:

"Chief! who comest uninvited, pratest in thy lying boast,
Thou shalt die the death of braggarts—witness be this mighty host!"

Karna answered calm and proudly, "Free this listed field to all,
Warriors enter by their prowess, wait not, Arjun, for thy call!

Warlike chieftains take their places by their strength of arm and might,
And their warrant is their falchion, valour sanctifies their right!

Angry word is coward's weapon, Arjun, speak with arrows keen,
Till I lay thee, witness Drona, low upon the listed green!"

Drona gave the word impartial, wrathful Arjun, dread of foes,
Parted from his loving brothers, with his glist'ning arms arose,

Karna clasped the Kuru's princes, parted from them one and all,
With his bow and ample quiver proudly stepped the warrior tall.

Now the clouds with lurid flashes gathered darkling, thick and high,
Lines of cranes like gleams of laughter sailed across the gloomy sky,

Rain-god INDRA over Arjun watched with father's partial love,
Watchful SURYA over Karna shed his light from far above,

Arjun stood in darkening shadow by the inky clouds concealed,
Bold and bright in open sunshine radiant Karna stood revealed!

Proud Duryodhan and his brothers stood by Karna calm and bold,
Drona stood by gallant Arjun, and brave Bhishma, warrior old,

Women too with partial glances viewed the one or other chief,
But by an equal love divided silent Pritha swooned in grief!

Wise Vidura, true to duty, with an anxious hurry came,
Sandal-drops and sprinkled water roused the woe-distracted dame,

And she saw her sons in combat, words of woe she uttered none,
Speechless wept, for none must fathom Karna was her eldest son!

VII

The Anointment of Karna

Crested Karna, helméd Arjun, proudly trod the spacious green,
Kripa, skilled in herald's duties, spake upon the dreadful scene:

"This is helmet-wearing Arjun, sprung of Kuru's mighty race,
Pandu's son and borne by Pritha, prince of worth and warlike grace,

Long-armed Chief! declare thy lineage, and the race thou dost adorn,
Name thy mother and thy father, and the house that saw thee born,

By the rules of war Prince Arjun claims his rival chief to know,
Princes may not draw their weapon 'gainst a base and nameless foe!"

Karna silent heard this mandate but his birth could not proclaim,
Like a raindrop-pelted lotus bent his humble head in shame!

Karna and Arjun.

"Prince we reckon," cried Duryodhan, "not the man of birth alone,
Warlike leader of his forces as a prince and chief we own!

Karna by his warlike valour is of crownéd kings the peer,
Karna shall be crownéd monarch, nations shall his mandate hear!"

Forth they brought the corn and treasure, golden coin and water jar,
On the throne they seated Karna famed in many a deathful war,

Brahmans chanted sacred *mantra* which the holy books ordain,
And anointed Karna monarch, king of Anga's fair domain!

And they raised the red umbrella, and they waved the *chowri* fan,
"Blessings on the crownéd monarch! honour to the bravest man!"

Now the holy rites accomplished, in his kingly robes arrayed
Karna unto prince Duryodhan thus in grateful accents prayed:

"Gift of kingdom, good Duryodhan, speaketh well thy noble heart,
What return can grateful Karna humbly render on his part?"

"Grant thy friendship," cries Duryodhan, "for no other boon I crave,
And Duryodhan's dearest comrade be thou Karna true and brave!"

"Be it so!" responded Karna, with a proud and noble grace,
And he sealed his loyal friendship in a dear and fond embrace!

VIII

The Chariot-driver

Wet with drops of toil and languor, lo! a chariot-driver came,
Loosely hung his scanty garments, and a staff upheld his frame,

Karna, now a crownéd monarch, to the humble charioteer,
Bent his head, still moist with water, as unto a parent dear!

With his scanty cloth the driver sought his dusty feet to hide,
And he hailed the gallant Karna as his son and as his pride,

And he clasped unto his bosom crownéd Karna's noble head,
And on Karna's dripping forehead, fresh and loving tear-drops shed!

Is he son of chariot-driver? Doubts arose in Bhima's mind,
And he sought to humble Karna with reproachful words unkind:

"Wilt thou, high-descended hero, with a Kuru cross thy brand?
But the goad of cattle-drivers better suits, my friend, thy hand!

Wilt thou as a crownéd monarch rule a mighty nation's weal?
As the jackals of the jungle sacrificial offerings steal!"

Quivered Karna's lips in anger, word of answer spake he none,
But a deep sigh shook his bosom, and he gazed upon the sun!

IX

Close of the Day

Like a lordly tusker rising from a beauteous lotus lake,
Rose Duryodhan from his brothers, proudly thus to Bhima spake:

"With such insults seek not, Bhima, thus to cause a warrior grief,
Bitter taunts but ill befit thee, warlike tiger-waisted chief!

Proudest chiefs may fight the humblest, for like river's noble course,
Noble deeds proclaim the warrior, and we question not their source!

Teacher Drona, priest and warrior, owns a poor and humble birth,
Kripa, noblest of Gautamas, springeth from the lowly earth!

Known to me thy lineage Bhima, thine and of thy brothers four,
Amorous gods your birth inspiréd, so they say, in days of yore!

Mark the great and gallant Karna decked in rings and weapons fair,
She-deer breeds not lordly tigers in her poor and lowly lair!

Karna comes to rule the wide earth, not fair Anga's realms alone,
By his valour and his weapons, by the homage which I own!

And if prince or arméd chieftain doth my word or deed gainsay,
Let him take his bow and quiver, meet me in a deadly fray!"

Loud applauses greet the challenge and the people's joyful cry,
But the thickening shades of darkness fill the earth and evening sky,

And the red lamp's fitful lustre shone upon the field around,
Slowly with the peerless Karna proud Duryodhan left the ground,

Pandu's sons with warlike Drona marked the darksome close of day,
And with Kripa and with Bhishma homeward silent bent their way.

"Arjun is the gallant victor!" "Valiant Karna's won the day!"
"Prince Duryodhan is the winner!" Various thus the people say.

By some secret sign apprised Pritha knew her gallant boy,
Saw him crownéd king of Anga with a mother's secret joy,

And with greater joy Duryodhan fastened Karna to his side,
Feared no longer Arjun's prowess, Arjun's skill of arms and pride,

E'en Yudhishthir reckoned Karna mightiest warrior on the earth,
Half misdoubted Arjun's prowess, Arjun's skill and warlike worth!

BOOK II

SWAYAMVARA

(*The Bride's Choice*)

THE mutual jealousies of the princes increased from day to day, and when Yudhishthir, the eldest of all the princes and the eldest son of the late king Pandu, was recognised heir-apparent, the anger of Duryodhan and his brothers knew no bounds. And they formed a dark scheme to kill the sons of Pandu.

The sons of Pandu were induced with their mother to pay a visit to a distant town called Varanavata. A house had been built there for their residence, constructed of inflammable materials. At the appointed time fire was set to the house; but the five brothers and their mother escaped the conflagration through a subterranean passage, retired into forests, and lived in the disgiuse of Brahmans.

In course of time they heard of the approaching celebration of the marriage of the princess of Panchala, an ancient kingdom in the vicinity of modern Kanouj. All the monarchs of Northern India were invited, and the bride would choose her husband from among the assembled kings according to the ancent *Swayamvara* custom. The five sons of Pandu decided to go and witness the ceremony.

The portion translated in this Book formed Sections clxxxiv. to cxxxix. of Book i. of the original text.

पृथा पाण्डवाश्च।

Pandavs journeying with their mother.

I

Journey to Panchala

Now the righteous sons of Pandu, wand'ring far from day to day,
Unto South Panchala's country glad and joyful held their way,

For when travelling with their mother, so it chanced by will of fate,
They were met by pious Brahmans bound for South Panchala's State,

And the pure and holy Brahmans hailed the youths of noble fame,
Asked them whither they would journey, from what distant land they came.

"From the land of Ekachakra," good Yudhishthir answered so,
"With our ancient mother travelling unto distant lands we go."

"Heard ye not," the Brahmans questioned, "in Panchala's fair domain,
Drupad, good and gracious monarch, doth a mighty feast ordain?

To that festive land we journey, Drupad's bounteous gifts to share,
And to see the *swayamvara* of Panchala's princess fair,—

Human mother never bore her, human bosom never fed,
From the Altar sprang the maiden who some noble prince will wed!

Soft her eyes like lotus-petal, sweet her tender jasmine form,
And a maiden's stainless honour doth her gentle soul inform!

And her brother, mailed and armèd with his bow and arrows dire,
Radiant as the blazing altar, sprang from Sacrificial Fire!

Fair the sister slender-waisted, dowered with beauty rich and rare,
And like fragrance of blue lotus, perfumes all the sweetened air!

She will chose from noble suitors gathered from the west and east,
Bright and fair shall be the wedding, rich and bounteous be the feast!

Kings will come from distant regions sacrificing wealth and gold,
Stainless monarchs versed in *sastra*, pious-hearted, mighty-souled,

Handsome youths and noble princes from each near and distant land,
Car-borne chieftains bold and skilful, brave of heart and stout of hand!

And to win the peerless princess they will scatter presents rare,
Food and milch-kine, wealth and jewels, gold and gifts and garments fair,

Noble gifts we take as Brahmans, bless the rite with gladsome heart,
Share the feast so rich and bounteous, then with joyful minds depart.

Actors, mimes and tuneful minstrels fair Panchala's court will throng,
Famed reciters of *puranas*, dancers skilled and wrestlers strong,

Come with us, the wedding witness, share the banquet rich and rare,
Pleased with gifts and noble presents to your distant home repair.

Dowered ye are with princely beauty, like the radiant gods above,
Even on you the partial princess may surrender heart and love!

And this youth so tall and stalwart, mighty-arméd, strong and bold,
He may win in feats of valour, and acquire much wealth and gold!"

"Be it so," Yudhishthir answered, "to Panchala we repair,
View the wedding of the princess and the royal bounty share."

Thus the righteous sons of Pandu with the Brahmans took their way,
Where in South Panchala's kingdom mighty Drupad held his sway.

Now the sinless saintly *rishi*, deathless bard of deathless lay,
Herald of the holy Vedas, Vyasa stood before their way!

And the princes bowed unto him and received his blessings kind,
By his mandate to Panchala went with pleased and joyful mind!

Jungle woods and silver waters round their sylvan pathway lay,
Halting at each wayside station marched the princes day by day,

Stainless and intent on *sastra*, fair in speech and pure in heart,
Travelling slow they reached Panchala, saw its spacious town and mart,

Saw the fort, bazaar and city, saw the spire and shining dome,
In a potter's distant cottage made their humble unknown home,

And disguised as pious Brahmans sons of Pandu begged their food,
People knew not Kuru's princes in that dwelling poor and rude.

II

The Wedding Assembly

To the helméd son of Pandu, Arjun pride of Kuru's race,
Drupad longed to give his daughter peerless in her maiden grace,

And of massive wood unbending, Drupad made a stubborn bow,
Saving Arjun prince or chieftain might not bend the weapon low,

And he made a whirling discus, hung it 'neath the open sky,
And beyond the whirling discus placed a target far and high,

"Whoso strings this bow," said Drupad, "hits the target in his pride,
Through the high and circling discus, he shall win Panchala's bride!"

And they spake the monarch's mandate in the kingdoms near and far,
And from every town and country princes came and chiefs of war,

Came the pure and saintly *rishis* for to bless the holy rite,
Came the Kurus with brave Karna in their pride and matchless might,

Brahmans came from distant regions with their sacred learning blest,
Drupad with a royal welcome greeted every honoured guest.

Now the festal day approacheth! Gathering men with ocean's voice,
Filled the wide and circling stages to behold the maiden's choice,

Royal guests and princely suitors came in pomp of wealth and pride,
Car-borne chiefs and mailéd warriors came to win the beauteous bride!

North-east of the festive city they enclosed a level ground,
Many a dome and stately palace cunning builders built around,

And by moat and wall surrounded, pierced by gate and archéd door,
By a canopy of splendour was the red field covered o'er!

Now the festive trumpets sounded and the censer fragrance lent,
Sprinkled *chandan* spread its coolness, wreaths were hung of sweetest scent,

All around were swan-white mansions, lofty domes and turrets high,
Like the peaks of white Kailasa cleaving through the azure sky!

Sparkling gems the chambers lighted, golden nets the windows laced,
Spacious stairs so wide and lofty were with beauteous carpets graced,

Rich festoons and graceful garlands gently waved like streamers gay,
And the swan-like silver mansions glinted in the light of day,

Gates below were thronged with people, far above the chambers lay,
With their lofty gilded turrets like the peaks of Himalay!

In these halls in pride and splendour dwelt each rich and royal guest,
Fired by mutual emulation, and in costly jewels drest,

Decked and perfumed sat these rulers, mighty-arméd, rich in fame,
Lion-monarchs, noble-destined, chiefs of pure and spotless name,

Pious to the mighty BRAHMA, and their subjects' hope and stay,
Loved of all for noble actions, kind and virtuous in their sway.

Now the festal day approacheth! like the heaving of the main,
Surge the ranks of gathered nations o'er the wide and spacious plain,

Pandu's sons in guise of Brahmans mix with Brahmans versed in lore,
Mark proud Drupad's wealth and splendour, gazing, wondering evermore!

Dancers charm the gathered people, singers sing and actors play,
Fifteen days of festive splendour greet the concourse rich and gay.

III

The Bride

Sound the drum and voice the *sankha!* Brightly dawns the bridal day,
Fresh from morning's pure ablutions comes the bride in garments gay!

And her golden bridal garland carries on her graceful arm,
Softly, sweetly, steps Draupadi, queen of every winning charm!

Then a Brahman versed in *mantra*, ancient priest of lunar race,
Lights the Fire, with pious offerings seeks its blessings and its grace,

Whispered words of benediction saints and holy men repeat,
Conch and trumpet's voice is silent, hushed the lofty war-drum's beat,

And there reigns a solemn silence, and in stately pomp and pride,
Drupad's son leads forth his sister, fair Panchala's beauteous bride!

In his loud and lofty accents like the distant thunder's sound,
Drupad's son his father's wishes thus proclaims to all around:

"*Mark this bow, assembled monarchs, and the target hung on high,*
Through yon whirling piercéd discus let five glist'ning arrows fly!

Whoso born of noble lineage, hits the far suspended aim,
Let him stand and as his guerdon Drupad's beauteous maiden claim!"

Then he turns unto Draupadi, tells each prince and suitor's name,
Tells his race and lofty lineage, and his warlike deeds of fame.

IV

The Suitors

"Brave Duryodhan and his brothers, princes of the Kuruland,
Karna proud and peerless archer, sister! seek thy noble hand,

And Gandhara's warlike princes, Bhoja's monarch true and bold,
And the son of mighty Drona, all bedecked in gems and gold!

King and prince from Matsya kingdom grace this noble wedding-feast,
Monarchs from more distant regions north and south and west and east,

Tamralipta and Kalinga on the eastern ocean wave,
Pattan's port whose hardy children western ocean's dangers brave!

From the distant land of Madra car-borne monarch Salya came,
And from Dwarka's sea-girt regions Valadeva known to fame,

Valadeva and his brother Krishna sprung from Yadu's race,
Of the Vrishni clan descended, soul of truth and righteous grace!

This is mighty Jayadratha come from Sindhu's sounding shore,
For his warlike feats renownéd, famed alike for sacred lore,

This is fair Kosala's monarch whose bright deeds our heralds sing,
From the sturdy soil of Chedi, Sisupala peerless king,

This is mighty Jarasandha, come from far Magadha's land,
These are other princely suitors, sister! eager for thy hand!

All the wide earth's warlike rulers seek to shoot the distant aim,
Princess, whoso hits the target, choose as thine that prince of fame!"

Decked with jewels, young and valiant, all aflame with soft desire,
Conscious of their worth and valour, all the suitors rose in ire,

Nobly born, of lofty presence, full of young unyielding pride,
Like the tuskers wild and lordly on Himalay's wooded side!

Each his rival marks as foeman as in field of deadly strife,
Each regards the fair Draupadi as his own his queenly wife,

On the gorgeous field they gather by a maddening passion fired,
And they strive as strove the bright gods, when by Uma's love
inspired!

And the gods in cloud-borne chariots came to view the scene so fair,
Bright ADITYAS in their splendour, MARUTS in the moving air,

Winged *suparnas*, scaly *nagas*, *deva-rishis* pure and high,
For their music famed, *gandharvas*, fair *apsaras* of the sky!

Valadeva armed with ploughshare, Krishna chief of righteous fame,
With the other Yadu chieftains to that wondrous bridal came,

Krishna marked the sons of Pandu eager for the queenly bride,
Like wild tuskers for a lotus, like the fire that ashes hide,

And he knew the warlike brothers in their holy Brahman guise,
Pointed them to Valadeva, gazing with a glad surprise!

But the other chiefs and monarchs with their eyes upon the bride,
Marked nor knew the sons of Pandu sitting speechless by their side,

And the long-armed sons of Pandu smitten by KANDARPA's dart,
Looked on her with longing languor and with love-impassioned heart!

Bright immortals gaily crowding viewed the scene surpassing fair,
Heavenly blossoms soft descending with a perfume filled the air,

Bright celestial cars in concourse sailed upon the cloudless sky,
Drum and flute and harp and tabor sounded deep and sounded high!

V

Trial of Skill

Uprose one by one the suitors, marking still the distant aim,
Mighty monarchs, gallant princes, chiefs of proud and warlike fame,

Decked in golden crown and necklace, and inflamed by pride and love,
Stoutly strove the eager suitors viewing well the targe above,

Strove to string the weapon vainly, tough unbending was the bow,
Slightly bent, rebounding quickly, laid the gallant princes low!

Strove the handsome suitors vainly, decked in gem and burnished gold,
Reft of diadem and necklace, fell each chief and warrior bold,

Reft of golden crown and garland, shamed and humbled in their pride,
Groaned the suitors in their anguish, sought no more Panchala's bride!

Uprose Karna, peerless archer, proudest of the archers he,
And he went and strung the weapon, fixed the arrows gallantly,

Stood like SURYA in his splendour and like AGNI in his flame,—
Pandu's sons in terror whispered, Karna sure must hit the aim!

But in proud and queenly accents Drupad's queenly daughter said:
"Monarch's daughter, born a Kshatra, Suta's son I will not wed!"

Karna heard with crimsoned forehead, left the emprise almost done,
Left the bow already circled, silent gazed upon the Sun!

Uprose Chedi's haughty monarch, mightiest of the monarchs he,
Other kings had failed inglorious, Sisupala stood forth free!

Firm in heart and fixed in purpose, bent the tough unbending bow,
Vainly! for the bow rebounding laid the haughty monarch low!

Uprose sturdy Jarasandha, fair Magadha's mighty chief,
Held the bow and stood undaunted, tall and stately as a cliff!

But once more the bow rebounded, fell the monarch in his shame,
Left in haste Panchala's mansions for the region whence he came!

Uprose Salya, king of Madra, with his wondrous skill and might,
Faltering, on his knees descending, fell in sad inglorious plight!

Thus each monarch fell and faltered, merry whispers went around,
And the sound of stifled laughter circled round the festive ground!

VI

The Disguised Arjun

Hushed the merry sound of laughter, hushed each suitor in his shame,
Arjun, godlike son of Pritha, from the ranks of Brahmans came!

Guised as Brahman young and holy and like INDRA's rainbow bright,
All the Brahmans shook their deerskins, cheered him in their
hearts' delight!

Some there were with sad misgivings heard the sound of joyous cheer,
And their minds were strangely anxious, whispered murmurs spake
their fear:

"Wondrous bow! which Sisupala, mighty Salya could not strain,
Jarasandha famed for prowess strove to bend and string in vain,

Can a Brahman weak by nature, and in warlike arms untrained,
Wield the bow which crownéd monarchs, long-armed chieftains
have not strained?

Sure the Brahman boy in folly dares a foolish thoughtless deed,
Shame amidst this throng of monarchs, shall it be the Brahman's
meed?

Youth in youthful pride or madness will a foolish emprise dare,
Sager men should stop his rashness and the Brahman's honour spare!"

"Shame he will not bring unto us," other Brahmans made reply,
"Rather in this throng of monarchs, rich renown and honour high,

Like a tusker strong and stately, like Himalay's towering crest,
Stands unmoved the youthful Brahman, ample-shouldered, deep in chest,

Lion-like his gait is agile, and determined is his air,
Trust me he can do an emprise who hath lofty will to dare!

He will do the feat of valour, will not bring disgrace and stain,
Nor is task in all this wide earth which a Brahman tries in vain!

Holy men subsist on wild fruits, in the strength of penance strong,
Spare in form, in spirit mightier than the mightiest warlike throng!

Ask not if 'tis right or foolish when a Brahman tries his fate,
If it leads to woe or glory, if 'tis mean or wondrous great!

Son of *rishi* Jamadagni baffled kings and chieftains high,
And Agastya stainless *rishi* drained the boundless ocean dry!

Let this young and daring Brahman undertake the warlike deed,
Let him try and by his prowess win the victor's noble meed!"

While the Brahmans deep revolving hopes and timid fears expressed,
By the bow the youthful Arjun stood unmoved like mountain crest!

Silent round the wondrous weapon thrice the mighty warrior went,
To the Lord of Gods, ISANA, in a silent prayer he bent!

Then the bow which gathered warriors vainly tried to bend and strain,
And the monarchs of the wide earth sought to string and wield in vain,

Godlike Arjun born of INDRA, filled with VISHNU's matchless might,
Bent the wondrous bow of Drupad, fixed the shining darts aright,

Through the disc the shining arrows fly with strange and hissing sound,
Hit and pierce the distant target, bring it thundering on the ground!

Shouts of joy and loud applauses Arjun's mighty feat declare,
Heavenly blossoms soft descended, heavenly music thrilled the air!

The Bride's Choice.

And the Brahmans shook their deerskins, but each irritated chief
In a lowly muttered whisper spake his rising rage and grief!

Sankha's note and voice of trumpet Arjun's glorious deed prolong,
Bards and heralds chant his praises in a proud and deathless song!

Drupad in the Brahman's mantle knew the hero proud and brave,
'Gainst the rage of baffled suitors sought the gallant prince to save,

With his twin-born youngest brothers left Yudhishthir, peaceful, good,
Bhima marked the gathering tempest and by gallant Arjun stood!

Like a queen the beauteous maiden now approached the archer brave,
Flung on him the bridal garland and the bridal robe she gave,

Arjun by his skill and prowess won Panchala's princess-bride,
People's shouts and Brahmans' blessings sounded joyful far and wide!

VII

The Tumult

Spake the suitors, anger-shaken, like a forest tempest-torn,
As Panchala's courteous monarch came to greet a Brahman-born:

"Shall he like the grass of jungle trample us in haughty pride,
To a prating priest and Brahman wed the proud and peerless bride?

To our hopes like nourished saplings shall he now the fruit deny?
Monarch proud who insults monarchs, sure a traitor's death shall die!

Honour for his rank we know not, have no mercy for his age,
Perish foe of crownéd monarchs, victim to our righteous rage!

Hath he asked us to his palace, favoured us with royal grace,
Feasted us with princely bounty but to compass our disgrace?

In this concourse of great monarchs, glorious like a heavenly band,
Doth he find no likely suitor for his beauteous daughter's hand?

And this rite of *swayamvara*, so our sacred laws ordain,
Is for warlike Kshatras only, priests that custom shall not stain!

If this maiden on a Brahman casts her eye, devoid of shame,
Let her expiate her folly in a pyre of blazing flame!

Leave the priestling in his folly sinning through a Brahman's greed,
For we wage no war with Brahmans and forgive a foolish deed!

Much we owe to holy Brahmans for our realm and wealth and life,
Blood of priest or wise preçeptor shall not stain our noble strife!

In the blood of sinful Drupad we the righteous laws maintain,
Such disgrace in future ages monarchs shall not meet again!"

Spake the suitors, tiger-hearted, iron-handed, bold and strong,
Fiercely bent on blood and vengeance blindly rose the maddened
throng!

On they came, the angry monarchs, armed for cruel vengeful strife,
Drupad midst the holy Brahmans trembling fled for fear of life!

Like wild elephants of jungle rushed the kings upon their foes,
Calm and stately, stalwart Bhima and the gallant Arjun rose!

With a wilder rage the monarchs viewed these brothers cross their path,
Rushed upon the daring warriors for to slay them in their wrath!

Weaponless was noble Bhima, but in strength like lightning's brand,
Tore a tree with peerless prowess, shook it as a mighty wand!

And the foe-compelling warrior held that mace of living wood,
Strong as Death with deadly weapon, facing all his foes he stood!

Arjun too with godlike valour stood unmoved, his bow in hand,
Side by side the dauntless brothers met a fierce and fiery band!

VIII

Krishna to the Rescue

Krishna knew the sons of Pandu though in robes of Brahmans dressed,
To his elder, Valadeva, thus his inner thoughts expressed:

"Mark that youth with bow and arrow and with lion's lordly gait,
He is helmet-wearing Arjun! greatest warrior midst the great!

Mark his mate, with tree uprooted how he meets the suitor band,
Save the tiger-waisted Bhima none can claim such strength of hand!

And the youth with eyes like lotus, he who left the court erewhile,
He is pious-souled Yudhishthir, man without a sin or guile!

And those youths beside Yudhisthir, Pandu's twin-born children they,
With her sons the righteous Pritha 'scaped where death and danger lay!

For the jealous, fierce Duryodhan darkly schemed their death by fire,
But the righteous sons of Pandu 'scaped Duryodhan's vengeful ire!"

Krishna rose amidst the monarchs, strove the tumult to appease,
And unto the angry suitors spake in words of righteous peace,

Monarchs bowed to Krishna's mandate, left Panchala's festive land,
Arjun took the beauteous princess, gently led her by the hand.

BOOK III

RAJASUYA

(The Imperial Sacrifice)

A CURIOUS incident followed the bridal of Draupadi. The five sons of Pandu returned with her to the potter's house, where they were living on alms according to the custom of Brahmans, and the brothers reported to their mother that they had received a great gift on that day. "Enjoy ye the gift in common," replied their mother, not knowing what it was. And as a mother's mandate cannot be disregarded, Draupadi became the common wife of the five brothers.

The real significance of this strange legend is unknown. The custom of brothers marrying a common wife prevails to this day in Thibet and among the hill-tribes of the Himalayas, but it never prevailed among the Aryan Hindus of India. It is distinctly prohibited in their laws and institutes, and finds no sanction in their literature, ancient or modern. The legend in the *Maha-bharata*, of brothers marrying a wife in common, stands alone and without a parallel in Hindu traditions and literature.

Judging from the main incidents of the Epic, Draupadi might rather be regarded as the wife of the eldest brother Yudhishthir. Bhima had already mated himself to a female in a forest, by whom he had a son, Ghatotkacha, who distinguished himself in war later on. Arjun too married the sister of Krishna, shortly after Draupadi's bridal, and had by her a son, Abhimanyu, who was one of the heroes of the war. On the other hand, Yudhishthir took to himself no wife save Draupadi, and she was crowned with Yudhishthir in the Rajasuya or Imperial Sacrifice. Notwithstanding the legend, therefore, Draupadi might be regarded as wedded to Yudhishthir, though won by the skill of Arjun, and this assumption would be in keeping with Hindu customs and laws, ancient and modern.

The jealous Duryodhan heard that his contrivance to kill his cousins at Varanavata had failed. He also heard that they had found a powerful friend in Drupad, and had formed an alliance with him. It was no longer possible to keep them from their rightful inheritance. The Kuru kingdom was accordingly parcelled; Duryodhan retained the eastern and richer portion with its ancient capital *Hastina-pura* on the Ganges; and the sons of Pandu were given the western portion on the Jumna, which was then a forest and a wilderness. The sons of Pandu cleared the forest and built a new capital *Indra-prastha*, the supposed ruins of which, near modern Delhi, are still pointed out to the curious traveller.

Yudhishthir the eldest of the five sons of Pandu, and now king of Indra-prastha, resolved to perform the Rajasuya sacrifice, which was a formal assumption of the Imperial title over all the kings of ancient India. His brothers went out with troops in all directions to proclaim his supremacy over all surrounding kings. Jarasandha, the powerful and semi-civilised king of Magadha or South Behar, opposed and was killed; but other monarchs recognised the supremacy of Yudhishthir and came to the sacrifice with tributes. King Dhrita-rashtra and his sons, now reigning at Hastina-pura, were politely invited to take a share in the performance of the sacrifice.

The portion translated in this Book forms Sections xxxiii. to xxxvi. and Section xliv. of Book ii. of the original.

I

The Assemblage of Kings

Ancient halls of proud Hastina! mirrored bright on Ganga's wave!
Thither came the son of Pandu, young Nakula, true and brave,

Came to ask Hastina's monarch, chief of Kuru's royal race,
To the feast of good Yudhishthir, and his sacrifice to grace,

Dhrita-rashtra came in gladness unto Indra-prastha's town,
Marked its new-built tower and turret on the azure Jumna frown,

With him came preceptor Kripa, and the ancient Bhishma came,
Elders of the race of Kuru, chiefs and Brahmans known to fame.

Monarchs came from distant regions to partake the holy rite,
Warlike chiefs from court and castle in their arms accoutred bright,

Kshatras came with ample tribute for the holy sacrifice,
Precious gems and costly jewels, gold and gifts of untold price.

Proud Duryodhan and his brothers, now repaired in friendly guise,
With the ancient Kuru monarch and Vidura good and wise,

With his son came brave Suvala from Gandhara's distant land,
Car-borne Salya, peerless Karna, came with bow and spear and brand.

Came the priest and proud preceptor Drona, skilled in arms and lore,
Jayadratha famed for valour came from Sindhu's sounding shore,

Drupad came with gallant princes from Panchala's land of fame,
Salwa lord of outer nations to the mighty gathering came.

Bhagadatta came in chariot from the land of nations brave,
Prag-jyotisha, where the red sun wakes on Brahma-putra's wave,

With him came untutored *mlechchas* who beside the ocean dwell,
Uncouth chiefs of dusky nations, from the lands where mountains
swell.

Came Virata, Matsya's monarch, and his warlike sons and bold,
Sisupala, king of Chedi, with his son bedecked in gold,

Came the warlike chiefs of Vrishni from the shores of Western Sea,
And the lords of Madhya-desa, ever warlike ever free!

II

Feast and Sacrifice

Jumna's dark and limpid waters laved Yudhishthir's palace walls,
And to hail him *Dharma-raja*, monarchs thronged his royal halls,

He to honoured kings and chieftains with a royal grace assigned
Palaces with sparkling waters, and with trees umbrageous lined,

Honoured thus, the mighty monarchs lived in mansions milky white,
Like the peaks of famed Kailasa lifting proud their snowy height!

Graceful walls that swept the meadows circled round the royal halls,
Nets of gold belaced the casements, gems bedecked the shining walls,

Flights of steps led up to chambers many-tinted-carpet-graced,
And festooning fragrant garlands were harmonious interlaced!

Far below from spacious gateways rose the people's gathering cry,
And from far the swan-white mansions caught the ravished gazer's
eye,

Richly graced with precious metals shone the turrets bright and gay,
Like the rich-ored shining turrets of the lofty Himalay!

And the scene bedecked by *rishis* and by priests and kings of might,
Shone like azure sky in splendour, graced by deathless Sons of Light!

Spake Yudhishthir unto Bhishma, elder of the Kuru race,
Unto Drona, proud preceptor, rich in lore and warlike grace,

Spake to wise preceptor Kripa versed in sacred rites of old,
To Duryodhan and his brothers, honoured guests and kinsmen bold:

"Friends and kinsmen, grant your favour and your sweet affection lend,
May your kindness ever helpful poor Yudhishthir's rite attend,

As your own, command my treasure, costly gifts and wealth untold,
To the poor and to the worthy scatter free my gems and gold!"

Speaking thus he made his *diksha*, and unto his work inclined,
To his friends and to his kinsmen all their various tasks assigned,

Proud Duhsasan in his bounty spreads the rich and sumptuous feast,
Drona's son with due devotion greets each saint and holy priest,

Sanjay with a regal honour welcomes king and chief of might,
Bhishma and the pious Drona watch the sacrificial rite,

Kripa guards the wealth and treasure, gold and gems of untold price,
And with presents unto Brahmans sanctifies the sacrifice,

Dhrita-rashtra, old and sightless, through the scene of gladness strays,
With a careful hand Vidura all the mighty cost defrays,

Proud Duryodhan took the tribute which the chiefs and monarchs paid,
Pious Krishna unto Brahmans honour and obeisance made.

'Twas a gathering fair and wondrous, on fair Jumna's sacred shore!
Tributes in a thousand *nishkas* every willing monarch bore,

Costly gifts proclaimed the homage of each prince of warlike might,
Chieftains vied with rival chieftains to assist the holy rite,

Bright Immortals, robed in sunlight, sailed across the liquid sky,
And their gleaming cloud-borne chariots rested on the turrets high!

Hero-monarchs, holy Brahmans filled the halls bedecked in gold,
White-robed priests adept in *mantra* mingled with the chieftains bold,

And amidst this scene of splendour, pious-hearted, pure and good,
Like the sinless god VARUNA, gentle-souled Yudhishthir stood!

Six bright fires Yudhishthir lighted, offerings made to gods above,
Gifts unto the poor and lowly spake the monarch's boundless love,

Hungry men were fed and feasted with an ample feast of rice,
Costly gifts to holy Brahmans graced the noble sacrifice,

Ida, *ajya*, *homa* offerings, pleased the "Shining Ones" on high,
Brahmans pleased with costly presents with their blessings filled
the sky!

III

Glimpses of the Truth

Dawned the day of *abhisheka*, proud anointment, sacred bath,
Crownéd kings and learnéd Brahmans crowded on Yudhishthir's path,

And as gods and heavenly *rishis* throng in Brahma's mansions bright,
Holy priests and noble monarchs graced the inner sacred site!

Measureless their fame and virtue, great their penance and their power,
And in converse deep and learned Brahmans passed the radiant hour,

And on subjects great and sacred, oft divided in their thought,
Various sages in their wisdom various diverse maxims taught,

Weaker reasons seemed the stronger, faultless reasons often failed,
Keen disputants like the falcon fell on views their rivals held!

Some were versed in Laws of Duty, some the Holy Vows professed,
Some with gloss and varied comment still his learned rival pressed,

Bright the concourse of the Brahmans unto sacred learning given,
Like the concourse of the bright stars in the glorious vault of heaven,

None of impure caste and conduct trespassed on the holy site,
None of impure life and manners stained Yudhishthir's sacred rite!

Deva-rishi, saintly Narad, marked the sacrificial rite,
Sanctifying by its lustre good Yudhishthir's royal might,

And a ray of heavenly wisdom lit the *rishi's* inner eye,
As he saw the gathered monarchs in the concourse proud and high!

He had heard from lips celestial in the heavenly mansions bright,
All these kings were gods incarnate, portions of Celestial Light!

And he saw in them embodied beings of the upper sky,
And in lotus-eyéd Krishna saw the Highest of the High!

Saw the ancient NARAYANA, great creation's Primal Cause,
Who had sent the gods as monarchs to uphold his righteous laws,

Battle for the cause of virtue, perish in a deadly war,
Then to seek their upper mansions in the radiant realms afar!

"NARAYANA, World's Preserver, sent immortal gods on earth,
He himself in race of Yadu hath assumed his mortal birth,

Like the moon among the planets born in Vrishni's noble clan,—
He whom bright gods render worship,—NARAYANA, Son of Man!

Primal Cause and Self-created! when is done his purpose high,
NARAYANA leads Immortals to their dwelling in the sky."

Such bright glimpses of the Secret came unto his inner sight,
As in lofty contemplation Narad gazed upon the rite.

IV

The Arghya

Outspake Bhishma to Yudhishthir: "Monarch of this wide domain,
Honour due to crownéd monarchs, doth our sacred law ordain,

Arghya to the wise Preceptor, to the Kinsman and to Priest,
To the Friend and to the Scholar, to the King as lord of feast,—

Unto these is due the *arghya*, so our holy writs have said,
Therefore to these kings assembled be the highest honour paid!

Noble are these crownéd monarchs, radiant like the noonday sun,
To the noblest, first in virtue, be the foremost honour done!"

"Who is noblest," quoth Yudhishthir, "in this galaxy of fame,
Who of chiefs and crownéd monarchs doth our foremost honour claim?"

Pond'ring spake the ancient Bhishma in his accents deep and clear:
"Greatest midst the great is Krishna! chief of men without a peer!

Midst these monarchs pure in lustre, purest-hearted and most high
Like the radiant sun is Krishna midst the planets of the sky!

Sunless climes are warmed to verdure by the sun's returning ray,
Windless wastes are waked to gladness when reviving breezes play!

Even so this *rajasuya*, holy sacrificial rite,
Owes its sanctity and splendour unto Krishna's holy might!"

Bhishma spake and Sahadeva served his mandate quick as thought,
And the *arghya* duly flavoured unto peerless Krishna brought,

Krishna trained in rules of virtue then the offered *arghya* took,
Darkened Sisupala's forehead and his frame in tremor shook!

To Yudhishthir and to Bhishma turns the chief his flaming eyes,
To the great and honoured Krishna, Sisupala wrathful cries.

V

Sisupala's Pride

"Not to Vrishni's uncrowned hero should this reverence be paid,
Midst these mighty crownéd monarchs in their kingly pomp arrayed!

Ill beseems the good Yudhishthir, royal Pandu's righteous son,
Homage to an uncrowned chieftain, to the lowly honour done!

Pandu's sons are yet untutored, and with knowledge yet unblessed;
Knowing Bhishma blessed with wisdom hath the rules of courts transgressed!

Learnéd in the Laws of Duty he hath sinned from partial love,
Conscious breach of rules of honour doth our deeper hatred move!

Midst these crownéd godlike monarchs, ruling kings of righteous fame,
Can this uncrowned Vrishni chieftain foremost rank and honour claim?

Doth he as a sage and elder claim the homage to him done?
Sure his father Vasudeva hath his claims before his son!

Doth he as Yudhishthir's kinsman count as foremost and the best?
Royal Drupad by alliance surely might the claim contest!

Doth he as a wise preceptor claim the highest, foremost place,
When the wise preceptor Drona doth this royal mansion grace?

Unto Krishna as a *rishi* should the foremost rank be given?
Saintly Vyasa claims the honour, Vedic bard inspired by Heaven!

Unto Krishna should we render honour for his warlike fame?
Thou O Bhishma! Death's Subduer, surely might precedence claim!

Unto Krishna for his knowledge should the noble prize we yield?
Drona's son unmatched in learning surely might contest the field!

Great Duryodhan midst the princes stands alone without a peer,
Kripa priest of royal Kurus, holiest of all priests is here!

Archer Karna!—braver archer none there is of mortal birth—
Karna learnt his arms from Rama, he who slew the kings of earth!

Wherefore then to unknown Krishna render we this homage free?
Saintly priest, nor wise preceptor, king nor foremost chief is he!"

VI

Sisupala's Fall

Tiger-hearted Sisupala spake in anger stern and high,
Calm unto him Krishna answered, but a light was in his eye :

" List O chiefs and righteous monarchs! from a daughter of our race
Evil-destined Sisupala doth his noble lineage trace,

Spite of wrong and frequent outrage, spite of insult often flung,
Never in his heart hath Krishna sought to do his kinsman wrong!

Once I went to eastern regions ; Sisupala like a foe
Burnt my far-famed seaport Dwarka, laid the mart and temple low!

Once on Bhoja's trusting monarch faithless Sisupala fell,
Slew his men and threw him captive in his castle's dungeon cell!

Once for holy *aswamedha* Vasudeva sent his steed,
Sisupala stole the charger, sought to stop the righteous deed!

Once on saintly Babhru's consort, pious-hearted, pure and just,
Sisupala fell in madness, forced the lady to his lust!

Once Visala's beauteous princess went to seek her husband's side,
In her husband's garb disguiséd Sisupala clasped the bride!

This and more hath Krishna suffered, for his mother is our kin,
But the sickening tale appalleth, and he addeth sin to sin!

One more tale of sin I mention : by his impious passion fired,
To my saintly wife, Rukmini, Sisupala hath aspired!

As the low-born seeks the *Veda*, soiling it with impure breath,
Sisupala sought my consort, and his righteous doom is Death ! "

Krishna spake; the rising red blood speaks each angry hero's shame,
Shame for Chedi's impious actions, grief for Sisupala's fame !

Loudly laughed proud Sisupala, spake with bitter taunt and jeer,
Answered Krishna's lofty menace with disdain and cruel sneer:

"Wherefore in this vast assembly thus proclaim thy tale of shame,
If thy wedded wife and consort did inspire my youthful flame?

Doth a man of sense and honour, blest with wisdom and with pride,
Thus proclaim his wedded consort was another's loving bride?

Do thy worst! Or if by anger or by thy forgiveness led,
Sisupala seeks no mercy, nor doth Krishna's anger dread!"

Lowered Krishna's eye and forehead, and unto his hands there came
Fatal disc, the dread of sinners, disc that never missed its aim!

"Monarchs in this hall assembled!" Krishna in his anger cried,
"Oft hath Chedi's impious monarch Krishna's noble rage defied,

For unto his pious mother plighted word and troth was given,
Sisupala's hundred follies would by Krishna be forgiven,

I have kept the plighted promise, but his crimes exceed the tale,
And beneath this vengeful weapon Sisupala now shall quail!"

Then the bright and whirling discus, as this mandate Krishna said,
Fell on impious Sisupala, from his body smote his head,

Fell the mighty-armèd monarch like a thunder-riven rock,
Severed from the parent mountain by the bolt's resistless shock!

And his soul be-cleansed of passions came forth from its mortal shroud,
Like the radiant sun in splendour from a dark and mantling cloud,

Unto Krishna good and gracious, like a lurid spark aflame,
Chastened of its sin and anger, soul of Sisupala came!

Rain descends in copious torrents, quick the lurid lightnings fly,
And the wide earth feels a tremor, restless thunders shake the sky!

Various feelings sway the monarchs as they stand in hushed amaze,
Mutely in those speechless moments on the lifeless warrior gaze,

Some there are who seek their weapons, and their nervous fingers shake,
And their lips they bite in anger, and their frames in tremor quake,

Others in their inmost bosom welcome Krishna's righteous deed,
Look on death of Sisupala as a sinner's proper meed,

Rishis bless the deed of Krishna as they wend their various ways,
Brahmans pure and pious-hearted chant the righteous Krishna's praise!

Sad Yudhisthir, gentle-hearted, thus unto his brothers said:
"Funeral rites and regal honours be performed unto the dead,"

Duteously his faithful brothers then performed each pious rite,
Honours due to Chedi's monarch, to his rank and peerless might,

Sisupala's son they seated in his mighty father's place,
And with holy *abhisheka* hailed him king of Chedi's race!

VII

Yudhishthir Emperor

Thus removed the hapless hindrance, now the holy sacrifice
Was performed with joy and splendour and with gifts of gold and rice,

Godlike Krishna watched benignly with his bow and disc and mace,
And Yudhishthir closed the feasting with his kindliness and grace.

Brahmans sprinkled holy water on the empire's righteous lord,
All the monarchs made obeisance, spake in sweet and graceful word:

"Born of race of Ajamidha! thou hast spread thy father's fame,
Rising by thy native virtue thou hast won a mightier name!

And this rite unto thy station doth a holier grace instil,
And thy royal grace and kindness all our hope and wish fulfil!

Grant us king of mighty monarchs! now unto our realms we go,
Emperor o'er earthly rulers! blessings and thy grace bestow!"

Then Yudhishthir to the monarchs parting grace and honours paid,
And unto his duteous brothers thus in loving-kindness said :

"To our feast these noble monarchs came from loyal love they bear,
Far as confines of their kingdoms, with them let our friends repair."

And his brothers and his kinsmen duteously his hest obey,
With each parting guest and monarch journey on the homeward way,

Arjun wends with high-souled Drupad, famed for lofty warlike grace,
Dhrishta-dyumna with Virata, monarch of the Matsya race,

Bhima on the ancient Bhishma and on Kuru's king doth wait,
Sahadeva waits on Drona, great in arms, in virtue great,

With Gandhara's warlike monarch brave Nakula holds his way,
Other chiefs with other monarchs where their distant kingdoms lay.

Last of all Yudhishthir's kinsman, righteous Krishna fain would part,
And unto the good Yudhishthir opens thus his joyful heart :

"Done this glorious *rajasuya*, joy and pride of Kuru's race!
Grant, O friend! to sea-girt Dwarka, Krishna now his steps must trace."

"By thy grace and by thy valour," sad Yudhishthir thus replies,
"By thy presence, noble Krishna! I performed this high emprise,

By thy all-subduing glory monarchs bore Yudhishthir's sway,
Came with gifts and costly presents, came their tributes rich to pay!

Must thou part? my uttered accents may not bid thee, friend, to go,
In thy absence vain were empire, and this life were full of woe,

Yet thou partest, sinless Krishna! dearest, best belovéd friend!
And to Dwarka's sea-washed mansions Krishna must his footsteps bend!"

Then unto Yudhishthir's mother, pious-hearted Krishna hies,
And in accents love-inspiring thus unto fair Pritha cries:

"Regal fame and righteous glory crown thy sons, reveréd dame!
Joy thee in their peerless prowess, in their holy, spotless fame!

May thy sons' success and triumph cheer a widowed mother's heart,
Grant me leave, O noble lady! for to Dwarka I depart."

From Yudhishthir's queen Draupadi, Krishna parts with many a tear,
And from Arjun's wife Subhadra, Krishna's sister ever dear!

Then the chief with due ablutions to the gods his offerings made,
Priests their sacred benedictions on the righteous Krishna laid,

And his faithful chariot-driver brought his falcon-bannered car,
Like the clouds in massive splendour, and resistless in the war,

Pious Krishna mounts the chariot, fondly greets his friends once more,
Leaves blue Jumna's sacred waters for his Dwarka's dear-loved shore.

Still Yudhishṭhir and his brothers, sad and sore and grieved at heart,
Followed Krishna's moving chariot, for they could not see him part,

Krishna stopped once more his chariot, and his parting blessings gave,
Thus the chief with eyes of lotus spake in accents calm and brave:

"*King of men! with sleepless watching, ever guard thy kingdom fair,*
Like a father tend thy subjects, with a father's love and care,

Be unto them like the rain-drop, nourishing the thirsty ground,
Be unto them tree of shelter, shading them from heat around,

Like the blue sky ever bending be unto them ever kind,
Anger-less and APRAMATTA, *rule them with a virtuous mind!*"

Spake and left the saintly Krishna, pure and pious-hearted chief,
Sad Yudhishthir wended homeward and his heart was filled with grief.

BOOK IV

DYUTA

(The Fatal Dice)

DURYODHAN came back from the Imperial Sacrifice filled with jealousy against Yudhishthir, and devised plans to effect his fall. Sakuni, prince of Gandhara, shared Duryodhan's hatred towards the sons of Pandu, and helped him in his dark scheme.

Yudhishthir with all his piety and righteousness had one weakness, the love of gambling, which was one of the besetting sins of the monarchs of the day. Sakuni was an expert at false dice, and challenged Yudhishthir, and Yudhishthir held it a point of honour not to decline such a challenge.

He came from his new capital, Indra-prastha, to Hastina-pura the capital of Duryodhan, with his mother and brothers and Draupadi. And as Yudhishthir lost game after game, he was stung with his losses, and with the recklessness of a gambler still went on with the fatal game. His wealth and hoarded gold and jewels, his steeds, elephants and cars, his slaves male and female, his empire and possessions, were all staked and lost!

The madness increased, and Yudhishthir staked his brothers, and then himself, and then the fair Draupadi, and lost! And thus the Emperor of Indra-prastha and his family were deprived of every possession on earth, and became the bond-slaves of Duryodhan. The old king Dhrita-rashtra released them from actual slavery, but the five brothers retired to forests as homeless exiles.

Portions of Section lxv. and the whole of Sections lxix., lxxvi., and lxxvii. of Book ii. of the original text have been translated in this Book.

I

Draupadi in the Council Hall

Glassed on Ganga's limpid waters brightly shine Hastina's walls!
Queen Draupadi duly honoured lives within the palace halls!

But as steals a lowly jackal in a lordly lion's den,
Base Duryodhan's humble menial came to proud Draupadi's ken.

"Pardon, Empress," quoth the menial, "royal Pandu's righteous son,
Lost his game and lost his reason, Empress, thou art staked and won!

Prince Duryodhan claims thee, lady, and the victor bids me say,
Thou shalt serve him as his vassal, as his slave in palace stay!"

"Have I heard thee, menial, rightly?" questioned she in anguish keen,
"Doth a crownéd king and husband stake his wife and lose his queen?

Did my noble lord and monarch sense and reason lose at dice,
Other stake he did not wager, wedded wife to sacrifice!"

"Other stakes were duly wagered," menial spake with bitter groan,
"Wealth and empire, every object which Yudhishthir called his own,

Lost himself and all his brothers, bondsmen are those princes brave,
Then he staked his wife and empress, thou art prince Duryodhan's
slave!"

Rose the queen in queenly anger, and with woman's pride she spake:
"Hie thee, menial, to thy master, Queen Draupadi's answer take!

If my lord, himself a bondsman, then hath staked his queen and wife,
False the stake, for owns a bondsman neither wealth nor other's life!

Slave can wager wife nor children, and such action is undone,
Take my word to prince Duryodhan, Queen Draupadi is unwon!"

In his fury heard Duryodhan fair Draupadi's message bold,
To his younger, wild Duhsasan, thus his angry mandate told:

"Little-minded is the menial, and his heart in terror fails,
For the fear of wrathful Bhima, lo! his coward-bosom quails!

Thou Duhsasan, bid the princess as our humble slave appear,
Pandu's sons are humble bondsmen, and thy heart it owns no fear!"

Fierce Duhsasan heard the mandate, blood-shot was his flaming eye,
Forthwith to the inner chambers with his eager steps did hie,

Proudly sat the fair Draupadi, monarch's daughter, monarch's wife,
Unto her the base Duhsasan spake the message, insult-rife:

"Lotus-eyed Panchala-princess! fairly staked and won at game,
Come and meet thy lord Duryodhan, chase that mantling blush of shame!

Serve us as thy lords and masters, be our beauteous bright-eyed slave,
Come unto the Council Chamber, wait upon the young and brave!"

Proud Draupadi shakes with tremor at Duhsasan's hateful sight,
And she shades her eye and forehead, and her bloodless cheeks are white,

At his words her chaste heart sickens, and with wild averted eye,
Unto rooms where dwelt the women, Queen Draupadi seeks to fly,

Vainly sped the trembling princess in her fear and in her shame,
By her streaming wavy tresses fierce Duhsasan held the dame!

Sacred locks! with holy water dewed at *rajasuya* rite,
And by *mantra* consecrated, fragrant, flowing, raven-bright,

Base Duhsasan by those tresses held the faint and flying queen,
Feared no more the sons of Pandu, nor their vengeance fierce and keen,

Dragged her in her slipping garments by her long and trailing hair,
And like sapling tempest-shaken, wept and shook the trembling fair!

Draupadis' Plaint.

Stooping in her shame and anguish, pale with wrath and woman's fear,
Trembling and in stifled accents, thus she spake with streaming tear :

"Leave me, shameless prince Duhsasan! elders, noble lords are here,
Can a modest wedded woman thus in loose attire appear?"

Vain the words and soft entreaty which the weeping princess made,
Vainly to the gods and mortals she in bitter anguish prayed!

For with cruel words of insult still Duhsasan mocked her woe:
"Loosely clad or void of clothing,—to the council hall you go!

Slave-wench fairly staked and conquered, wait upon thy masters brave,
Live among our household menials, serve us as our willing slave!"

II

Draupadi's Plaint

Loose-attired, with trailing tresses, came Draupadi weak and faint,
Stood within the Council Chamber, tearful made her piteous plaint:

"Elders! versed in holy *sastra*, and in every holy rite,
Pardon if Draupadi cometh in this sad unseemly plight!

Stay thy sinful deed, Duhsasan, nameless wrongs and insults spare,
Touch me not with hands uncleanly, sacred is a woman's hair!

Honoured elders, righteous nobles, have on me protection given,
Tremble sinner, seek no mercy from the wrathful gods in heaven!

Here in glory, son of Dharma, sits my noble righteous lord,
Sin nor shame nor human frailty stains Yudhishthir's deed or word!

Silent all? and will no chieftain rise to save a woman's life?
Not a hand or voice is lifted to defend a virtuous wife?

Lost is Kuru's righteous glory, lost is Bharat's ancient name,
Lost is Kshatra's kingly prowess, honour, worth and knightly fame!

Wherefore else do Kuru warriors tamely view this impious scene,
Wherefore gleam not righteous weapons to protect an outraged queen?

Bhishma, hath he lost his virtue, Drona, hath he lost his might,
Hath the monarch of the Kurus ceased to battle for the right?

Wherefore are ye mute and voiceless, councillors of mighty fame?
Vacant eye and palsied right arm watch this deed of Kuru's shame!"

III

Insult and Vow of Revenge

Spake Draupadi slender-waisted, and her words were stern and high,
Anger flamed within her bosom and the tear was in her eye!

And her sparkling, speaking glances fell on Pandu's sons like fire,
Stirred in them a mighty passion and a thirst for vengeance dire!

Lost their empire, wealth and fortune, littled recked they for the fall,
But Draupadi's pleading glances like a poniard smote them all!

Darkly frowned the ancient Bhishma, wrathful Drona bit his tongue,
Pale Vidura marked with anger insults on Draupadi flung!

Fulsome word nor foul dishonour could their truthful utterance taint,
And they blamed Duhsasan's action, when they heard Draupadi's
plaint!

But brave Karna, though a warrior,—Arjun's deadly foe was he,—
'Gainst the humbled sons of Pandu spake his scorn thus bitterly:

"'Tis no fault of thine, fair princess! fallen to this servile state,
Wife and son rule not their actions, others rule their hapless fate!

Thy Yudhishthir sold his birthright, sold thee at the impious play,
And the wife falls with the husband, and her duty—to obey!

Live thou in this Kuru household, do the Kuru princes' will,
Serve them as thy lords and masters, with thy beauty please them still!

Fair One! seek another husband who in foolish reckless game
Will not stake a loving woman, will not cast her forth in shame!

For they censure not a woman, when she is a menial slave,
If her woman's fancy wanders to the young and to the brave!

For thy lord is not thy husband, as a slave he hath no wife,
Thou art free with truer lover to enjoy a wedded life!

They whom at the *swayamvara*, chose ye, fair Panchala's bride,
They have lost thee, sweet Draupadi, lost their empire and their pride!"

Bhima heard, and quick and fiercely heaved his bosom in his shame,
And his red glance fell on Karna like a tongue of withering flame!

Bound by elder's plighted promise Bhima could not smite in ire,
Looked a painted form of Anger flaming with an anguish dire!

"King and elder!" uttered Bhima, and his words were few and brave,
"Vain were wrath and righteous passion in the sold and bounden slave!

Would that son of chariot-driver fling on us this insult keen,
Hadst thou, noble king and elder, staked nor freedom nor our queen?"

Sad Yudhishthir heard in anguish, bent in shame his lowly head,
Proud Duryodhan laughed in triumph, and in scornful accents said:

"Speak, Yudhishthir, for thy brothers own their elder's righteous sway,
Speak, for truth in thee abideth, virtue ever marks thy way,

Hast thou lost thy new-built empire and thy brothers proud and brave?
Hast thou lost thy fair Draupadi, is thy wedded wife our slave?"

Lip nor eye did move Yudhishthir, hateful truth would not deny,
Karna laughed, but saintly Bhishma wiped his old and manly eye!

Madness seized the proud Duryodhan, and inflamed by passion base,
Sought the prince to stain Draupadi with a deep and foul disgrace!

On the proud and peerless woman cast his loving, lustful eye,
Sought to hold the high-born princess as his slave upon his knee!

Bhima penned his wrath no longer, lightning-like his glance he flung,
And the ancient hall of Kurus with his thunder accents rung:

"*May I never reach those mansions where my fathers live on high,
May I never meet ancestors in the bright and happy sky,*

*If that knee, by which thou sinnest, Bhima breaks not in his ire,
In the battle's red arena with his weapon, deathful, dire!*"

Red fire flamed on Bhima's forehead, sparkled from his angry eye,
As from tough and gnarléd branches fast the crackling red sparks fly!

IV

Dhrita-rashtra's Kindness

Hark! within the sacred chamber, where the priests in white attire
With libations morn and evening feed the sacrificial fire,

And o'er sacred rites of *homa* Brahmans chant their *mantra* high,
There is heard the jackal's wailing and the raven's ominous cry!

Wise Vidura knew that omen, and the Queen Gandhari knew,
Bhishma muttered "*svasti! svasti!*" at this portent strange and new,

Drona and preceptor Kripa uttered too that holy word,
Spake her fears the Queen Gandhari to her spouse and royal lord.

Dhrita-rashtra heard and trembled with a sudden holy fear,
And his feeble accents quavered, and his eyes were dimmed by tear:

"Son Duryodhan, ever luckless, godless, graceless, witless child,
Hast thou Drupad's virtuous daughter thus insulted and reviled?

Hast thou courted death and danger, for destruction clouds our path?
May an old man's soft entreaties still avert this sign of wrath!"

Slow and gently to Draupadi was the sightless monarch led,
And in kind and gentle accents unto her the old man said:

"Noblest empress, dearest daughter, good Yudhishthir's stainless wife,
Purest of the Kuru ladies, nearest to my heart and life!

Pardon wrong and cruel insult and avert the wrath of Heaven,
Voice thy wish and ask for blessing, be my son's misdeed forgiven!"

Answered him the fair Draupadi: "Monarch of the Kuru's line,
For thy grace and for thy mercy every joy on earth be thine!

Since thou bid'st me name my wishes, this the boon I ask of thee,
That my gracious lord Yudhishthir once again be bondage-free!

I have borne a child unto him, noble boy and fair and brave,
Be he prince of royal station, not the son of bounden slave!

Let not light unthinking children point to him in utter scorn,
Call him slave and *dasaputra*, of a slave and bondsman born!"

"Virtuous daughter, have thy wishes," thus the ancient monarch cried,
"Name a second boon and blessing, and it shall be gratified."

"Grant me then, O gracious father! mighty Bhima, Arjun brave,
And the youngest twin-born brothers,—none of them may be a slave!

With their arms and with their chariots let the noble princes part,
Freemen let them range the country, strong of hand and stout of heart!"

"Be it so! high-destined princess!" ancient Dhrita-rashtra cried,
"Name another boon and blessing, and it shall be gratified.

Foremost of my queenly daughters, dearest-cherished and the best,
Meeting thus thy gentle wishes, now I feel my house is blest!"

"Not so," answered him the princess, "other boon I may not seek,
Thou art bounteous, and Draupadi should be modest, wise and meek,

Twice I asked, and twice you granted, and a Kshatra asks no more,
Unto Brahmans it is given, asking favours evermore!

Now my lord and warlike brothers, from their hateful bondage freed,
Seek their fortune by their prowess and by brave and virtuous deed!"

V

The Banishment

Now Yudhishthir 'reft of empire, far from kinsmen, hearth and home,
With his wife and faithful brothers must as houseless exiles roam.

Parting blessing spake Yudhishthir, "Elder of the Kuru line!
Noble grandsire, stainless Bhishma! may thy glories ever shine!

Drona, priest and great preceptor! saintly Kripa true and brave!
Kuru's monarch Dhrita-rashtra! may the gods thy empire save!

Good Vidura true and faithful! may thy virtue serve thee well!
Warlike sons of Dhrita-rashtra! let me bid you all farewell!"

So he spake unto his kinsmen, wishing good for evil done,
And in silent shame they listened, parting words they uttered none!

Pained at heart was good Vidura, and he asked in sore distress:
"*Arya* Pritha, will she wander in the pathless wilderness?

Royal-born, unused to hardship, weak and long unused to roam,
Agéd is thy saintly mother, let fair Pritha stay at home.

And by all beloved, respected, in my house shall Pritha dwell,
Till your years of exile over, ye shall greet her safe and well."

Answered him the sons of Pandu: "Be it even as you say,
Unto us thou art a father, we thy sacred will obey,

Give us then thy holy blessings, friend and father! ere we part,
Blessings from the true and righteous brace the feeble, fainting heart."

Spake Vidura, pious-hearted: "Best of Bharat's ancient race,
Let me bless thee and thy brothers, souls of truth and righteous grace!

Fortune brings no weal to mortals who may win by wicked wile,
Sorrow brings no shame to mortals who are free from sin and guile!

Thou art trained in laws of duty, Arjun is unmatched in war,
And on Bhima in the battle kindly shines his faithful star,

And the Twins excel in wisdom, born to rule a mighty State,
Fair Draupadi, ever faithful, wins the smiles of fickle Fate!

Each with varied gifts endowéd, each beloved of one and all,
Ye shall win a spacious empire, greater, mightier, after fall,

This your exile, good Yudhishthir, is ordained to serve your weal,
Is a trial and *samadhi*, for it chastens but to heal!

Meru taught thee righteous maxims where Himalay soars above,
And in Varnavata's forest Vyasa taught thee holy love,

Rama preached the laws of duty on fair Bhrigu's lofty hill,
Sambhu showed the 'way' where floweth Drisad-vati's limpid rill,

Fell from lips of saint Asita, words of wisdom deep and grave,
Bhrigu touched with fire thy bosom by the dark Kalmashi's wave,

Now once more the teaching cometh, purer, brighter, oftener taught,
Learn the truth from heavenly Narad, happy is thy mortal lot!

Greater than the son of Ila, than the kings of earth in might,
Holier than the holy *rishis*, be thou in thy virtue bright!

INDRA help thee in thy battles, proud subduer of mankind,
YAMA in the mightier duty, in the conquest of thy mind!

Good KUVERA teach thee kindness, hungry and the poor to feed,
King VARNUA quell thy passions, free thy heart from sin and greed!

Like the Moon in holy lustre, like the Earth in patience deep,
Like the Sun be full of radiance, strong like wind's resistless sweep!

In thy sorrow, in affliction, ever deeper lessons learn,
Righteous be your life in exile, happy be your safe return!

May these eyes again behold thee in Hastina's ancient town,
Conqueror of earthly trials, crowned with virtue's heavenly crown!"

Spake Vidura to the brothers, and they felt their might increase,
Bowed to him in salutation, filled with deeper, holier peace,

Bowed to Bhishma and to Drona, and to chiefs and elders all,
Exiles to the pathless jungle left their father's ancient hall!

VI

Pritha's Lament

In the inner palace chambers where the royal ladies dwell,
Unto Pritha came Draupadi, came to speak her sad farewell,

Monarch's daughter, monarch's consort, as an exile she must go,
Pritha wept and in the chambers rose the wailing voice of woe!

Heaving sobs convulsed her bosom as a silent prayer she prayed,
And in accents choked by anguish thus her parting words she said:

"Grieve not, child, if bitter fortune so ordains that we must part,
Virtue hath her consolations for the true and loving heart!

And I need not tell thee, daughter, duties of a faithful wife,
Drupad's and thy husband's mansions thou hast brightened by the life!

Nobly from the sinning Kurus thou hast turned thy righteous wrath,
Safely, with a mother's blessing, tread the trackless jungle path!

Dangers bring no woe or sorrow to the true and faithful wife,
Sinless deed and holy conduct ever guard her charméd life!

Nurse thy lord with woman's kindness, and his brothers, where ye go,
Young in years is Sahadeva, gentle and unused to woe!"

"Thy fond blessings help me, mother," so the fair Draupadi said,
"Safe in righteous truth and virtue, forest paths we fearless tread!"

Wet her eyes and loose her tresses, fair Draupadi bowed and left,
Ancient Pritha weeping followed of all earthly joy bereft,

As she went, her duteous children now before their mother came,
Clad in garments of the deer-skin, and their heads were bent in shame!

Sorrow welling in her bosom choked her voice and filled her eye,
Till in broken stifled accents faintly thus did Pritha cry:

"Ever true to path of duty, noble children void of stain,
True to gods, to mortals faithful, why this unmerited pain?

Wherefore hath untimely sorrow like a darksome cloud above,
Cast its pale and deathful shadow on the children of my love?

Woe to me, your wretched mother, woe to her who gave you birth,
Stainless sons, for sins of Pritha have ye suffered on this earth!

Shall ye range the pathless forest dreary day and darksome night,
Reft of all save native virtue, clad in native, inborn might?

Woe to me, from rocky mountains where I dwelt by Pandu's side,
When I lost him, to Hastina wherefore came I in my pride?

Happy is your sainted father; dwells in regions of the sky,
Sees nor feels these earthly sorrows gathering on us thick and high!

Happy too is faithful Madri; for she trod the virtuous way,
Followed Pandu to the bright sky, and is now his joy and stay!

Ye alone are left to Pritha, dear unto her joyless heart,
Mother's hope and widow's treasure, and ye may not, shall not part!

Leave me not alone on wide earth, loving sons your virtues prove,
Dear Draupadi, loving daughter, let a mother's tear-drops move!

Grant me mercy, kind Creator, and my days in mercy close,
End my sorrows, kind VIDHATA, end my life with all my woes!

Help me, pious-hearted Krishna, friend of friendless, wipe my pain,
All who suffer pray unto thee and they never pray in vain!

Help me, Bhishma, warlike Drona, Kripa ever good and wise,
Ye are friends of truth and virtue, righteous truth ye ever prize!

Help me from thy starry mansions, husband, wherefore dost thou wait,
Seest thou not thy godlike children exiled by a bitter fate!

Part not, leave me not, my children, seek ye not the trackless way,
Stay but one, if one child only, as your mother's hope and stay!

Youngest, gentlest Sahadeva, dearest to this widowed heart,
Wilt thou watch beside thy mother, while thy cruel brothers part?"

Whispering words of consolation, Pritha's children wiped her eye,
Then unto the pathless jungle turned their steps with bitter sigh!

Kuru dames with fainting Pritha to Vidura's palace hie,
Kuru queens for weeping Pritha raise their voice in answering cry,

Kuru maids for fair Draupadi fortune's fitful will upbraid,
And their tear-dewed lotus-faces with their streaming fingers shade!

Dhrita-rashtra, ancient monarch, is by sad misgivings pained,
Questions oft with anxious bosom what the cruel fates ordained.

BOOK V

PATIVRATA-MAHATMYA

(Woman's Love)

TRUE to their word the sons of Pandu went with Draupadi to exile, and passed twelve years in the wilderness; and many were the incidents which checkered their forest life. Krishna, who had stood by Yudhishthir in his prosperity, now came to visit him in his adversity; he consoled Draupadi in her distress, and gave good advice to the brothers. Draupadi with a woman's pride and anger still thought of her wrongs and insults, and urged Yudhishthir to disregard the conditions of exile and recover his kingdom. Bhima too was of the same mind, but Yudhishthir would not be moved from his plighted word.

The great *rishi* Vyasa came to visit Yudhishthir, and advised Arjun, great archer as he was, to acquire celestial arms by penance and worship. Arjun followed the advice, met the god SIVA in the guise of a hunter, pleased him by his prowess in combat, and obtained his blessings and the *pasupata* weapon. Arjun then went to INDRA's heaven and obtained other celestial arms.

In the meanwhile Duryodhan, not content with sending his cousins to exile, wished to humiliate them still more by appearing before them in all his regal power and splendour. Matters however turned out differently from what he expected, and he became involved in a quarrel with some *gandharvas*, a class of aerial beings. Duryodhan was taken captive by them, and it was the Pandav brothers who released him from his captivity, and allowed him to return to his kingdom in peace. This act of generosity rankled in his bosom and deepened his hatred.

Jayadratha, king of the Sindhu or Indus country, and a friend and ally of Duryodhan, came to the woods, and in the absence of the Pandav brothers carried off Draupadi. The Pandavs however pursued the king, chastised him for his misconduct, and rescued Draupadi.

Still more interesting than these various incidents are the tales and legends with which this book is replete. Great saints came to see Yudhishthir in his exile, and narrated to him legends of ancient times and of former kings. One of these beautiful episodes, the tale of Nala and Damayanti, has been translated into graceful English verse by Dean Milman, and is known to many English readers. The legend of Agastya who drained the ocean dry; of Parasu-Rama a Brahman who killed the Kshatriyas of the earth; of Bhagiratha who brought down the Ganges from the skies to the earth; of Manu and the universal deluge; of Vishnu and various other gods; of Rama and his deeds which form the subject of the Epic *Ramayana*;—these and various other legends have been interwoven in the account of the forest-life of the Pandavs, and make it a veritable storehouse of ancient Hindu tales and traditions.

Among these various legends and tales I have selected one which is singular and striking. The great truth proclaimed under the thin guise of an eastern allegory is that a True Woman's Love is not conquered by Death. The story is known by Hindu women high and low, rich and poor, in all parts of India; and on a certain night in the year millions of Hindu women celebrate a rite in honour of the woman whose love was not conquered by death. Legends like these, though they take away from the unity and conciseness of the Epic, impart a moral instruction to the millions of India the value of which cannot be overestimated.

The portion translated in this Book forms Sections ccxcii. and ccxciii., a part of Section ccxciv. and Sections ccxcv. and ccxcvi. of Book iii. of the original text.

I

Forest Life

In the dark and pathless forest long the Pandav brothers strayed,
In the bosom of the jungle with the fair Draupadi stayed,

And they killed the forest red-deer, hewed the gnarlèd forest wood,
From the stream she fetched the water, cooked the humble daily food,

In the morn she swept the cottage, lit the cheerful fire at eve,
But at night in lonesome silence oft her woman's heart would grieve,

Insults rankled in her bosom and her tresses were unbound,—
So she vowed,—till fitting vengeance had the base insulters found!

Oft when evening's shades descended, mantling o'er the wood and lea,
When Draupadi by the cottage cooked the food beneath the tree,

Rishis came to good Yudhishthir, sat beside his evening fires,
Many olden tales recited, legends of our ancient sires.

Markandeya, holy *rishi*, once unto Yudhishthir came,
When his heart was sorrow-laden with the memories of his shame,

"Pardon, rishi!" said Yudhishthir, "if unbidden tears will start,
But the woes of fair Draupadi grieve a banished husband's heart!

By her tears the saintly woman broke my bondage worse than death,
By my sins she suffers exile and misfortune's freezing breath!

Dost thou, sage and saintly *rishi*, know of wife or woman born,
By such nameless sorrow smitten, by such strange misfortune torn?

Hast thou in thy ancient legends heard of true and faithful wife,
With a stronger wife's affection, with a sadder, bitterer life?"

"Listen, monarch!" said the *rishi*, "to a tale of ancient date,
How Savitri loved and suffered, how she strove and conquered Fate!"

II

The Tale of Savitri

In the conntry of the Madras lived a king in days of old,
Faithful to the holy BRAHMA, pure in heart and righteous-souled,

He was loved in town and country, in the court and hermit's den,
Sacrificer to the bright gods, helper to his brother men,

But the monarch, Aswapati, son or daughter had he none,
Old in years and sunk in anguish, and his days were almost done!

Vows he took and holy penance, and with pious rules conformed,
Spare in diet as *brahmachari* many sacred rites performed,

Sang the sacred hymn, *savitri*, to the gods oblations gave,
Through the livelong day he fasted, uncomplaining, meek and brave!

Year by year he gathered virtue, rose in merit and in might,
Till the goddess of *savitri* smiled upon his sacred rite,

From the fire upon the altar, which a holy radiance flung,
In the form of beauteous maiden, goddess of *savitri* sprung!

And she spake in gentle accents, blessed the monarch good and brave,
Blessed his rites and holy penance and a boon unto him gave:

"Penance and thy sacrifices can the powers immortal move,
And the pureness of thy conduct doth thy heart's affection prove,

Ask thy boon, king Aswapati, from creation's Ancient Sire,
True to virtue's sacred mandate speak thy inmost heart's desire!"

"For an offspring brave and kingly," so the saintly king replied,
"Holy rites and sacrifices and this penance I have tried,

If these rites and sacrifices move thy favour and thy grace,
Grant me offspring, Prayer-Maiden, worthy of my noble race!"

"Have thy object," spake the Maiden, "Madra's pious-hearted king,
From SWAYMBHU, Self-created, blessings unto thee I bring!

For HE lists to mortal's prayer springing from a heart like thine,
And HE wills,—a noble daughter grace thy famed and royal line!

Aswapati, glad and grateful, take the blessing which I bring,
Part in joy and part in silence, bow unto Creation's King!"

Vanished then the Prayer-Maiden, and the king of noble fame,
Aswapati, Lord of coursers, to his royal city came,

Days of hope and nights of gladness Madra's happy monarch passed,
Till his queen of noble offspring gladsome promise gave at last!

As the moon each night increaseth, chasing darksome nightly gloom,
Grew the unborn babe in splendour in its happy mother's womb,

And in fulness of the season came a girl with lotus-eye,
Father's hope and joy of mother, gift of kindly gods on high!

And the king performed its birth-rites with a glad and grateful mind,
And the people blessed the dear one with their wishes good and kind,

As *Savitri*, Prayer-Maiden, had the beauteous offspring given,
Brahmans named the child *Savitri*, holy gift of bounteous Heaven!

Grew the child in brighter beauty like a goddess from above,
And each passing season added fresher sweetness, deeper love,

Came with youth its lovelier graces, as the buds their leaves unfold,
Slender waist and rounded bosom, image as of burnished gold,

Deva-Kanya! born a goddess, so they said in all the land,
Princely suitors struck with splendour ventured not to seek her hand!

Once upon a time it happened on a bright and festive day,
Fresh from bath the beauteous maiden to the altar came to pray,

And with cakes and pure libations duly fed the Sacred Flame,
Then like SRI in heavenly radiance to her royal father came,

Bowed unto his feet in silence, sacred flowers beside him laid,
And her hands she folded meekly, sweetly her obeisance made,

With a father's pride, upon her gazed the ruler of the land,
But a strain of sadness lingered, for no suitor claimed her hand!

"Daughter," whispered Aswapati, "now, methinks, the time is come,
Thou shouldst choose a princely suitor, grace a royal husband's home,

Choose thyself a noble husband worthy of thy noble hand,
Choose a true and upright monarch, pride and glory of his land,

As thou choosest, gentle daughter, in thy loving heart's desire,
Blessing and his sweet permission will bestow thy happy sire!

For our sacred *sastras* sanction, holy Brahmans oft relate,
That the duty-loving father sees his girl in wedded state,

That the duty-loving husband watches o'er his consort's ways,
That the duty-loving offspring tends his mother's widowed days,

Do thou therefore choose a husband, daughter of my house and love,
So thy father earn no censure or from men or gods above!"

Fair Savitri bowed unto him, and for parting blessings prayed,
Then she left her father's palace, and in distant regions strayed,

With her guard and aged courtiers whom her watchful father sent,
Mounted on her golden chariot unto sylvan woodlands went.

Then in pleasant wood and jungle wandered she from day to day,
Unto *asrams*, hermitages, pious-hearted held her way,

Oft she stayed in holy *tirthas* washed by sacred limpid streams,
Food she gave unto the hungry, wealth beyond their fondest dreams!

Many days and months are over, and it once did so befall,
When the king and *rishi* Narad sat within the royal hall,

From her journeys near and distant and from places known to fame,
Fair Savitri with the courtiers to her father's palace came,

And she saw her royal father, *rishi* Narad by his seat,
Bent her head in salutation, bowed unto their holy feet.

III

The Fated Bridegroom

"Whence comes she," so Narad questioned, "whither was Savitri led,
Wherefore to a happy husband hath Savitri not been wed?"

"Nay! to choose her lord and husband," so the virtuous monarch said,
"Fair Savitri long hath wandered and in holy *tirthas* stayed,

Maiden! speak unto the *rishi*, and thy choice and secret tell!"
Then a blush suffused her forehead, soft and slow her accents fell!

"Listen, father! Salwa's monarch was of old a king of might,
Righteous-hearted Dyumat-sena, feeble now and void of sight,

Foemen robbed him of his kingdom when in age he lost his sight,
And from town and spacious empire was the monarch forced to flight,

With his queen and with his infant did the feeble monarch stray,
And the jungle was his palace, darksome was his weary way.

Holy vows assumed the monarch and in penance passed his life,
In the wild woods nursed his infant and with wild fruits fed his wife,

Years have gone in rigid penance, and that child is now a youth,
Him I choose my lord and husband, Prince Satyavan, Soul of
 Truth!"

Thoughtful was the *rishi* Narad, doleful were the words he said:
"Sad disaster waits Savitri if this royal youth she wed!

Truth-beloving is his father, truthful is the royal dame,
Truth and virtue rule his actions, and Satyavan is his name,

Steeds he loved in days of boyhood and to paint them was his joy,
Hence they called him young Chitraswa, art-beloving gallant boy!

But O pious-hearted monarch! fair Savitri hath in sooth
Courted Fate and sad disaster in that noble gallant youth!"

"Tell me," questioned Aswapati, "for I may not guess thy thought,
Wherefore is my daughter's action with a sad disaster fraught?

Is the youth of noble lustre, gifted in the gifts of art,
Blest with wisdom, prowess, patience, daring, dauntless in his heart?"

"SURYA's lustre in him shineth," so the *rishi* Narad said,
"BRIHASPATI's wisdom dwelleth in the young Satyavan's head,

Like MAHENDRA in his prowess, and in patience like the Earth,
Yet O king! a sad disaster marks the gentle youth from birth!"

"Tell me, *rishi*, then thy reason," so the anxious monarch cried,
"Why to youth so great and gifted may this maid be not allied?

Is Satyavan free in bounty, gentle-hearted, full of grace,
Duly versed in sacred knowledge, fair in mind and fair in face?"

"Free in gifts like Rantideva," so the holy *rishi* said,
"Versed in lore like monarch Sivi, who all ancient monarchs led,

Like Yayati open-hearted, and like CHANDRA in his grace,
Like the handsome heavenly ASVINS, fair and radiant is his face,

Meek and graced with patient virtue, he controls his noble mind,
Modest in his kindly actions, true to friends and ever kind,

And the hermits of the forest praise him for his righteous truth,
Nathless, king, thy daughter may not wed this noble-hearted youth!"

"Tell me, *rishi*," said the monarch, "for thy sense from me is hid,
Has this prince some fatal blemish? wherefore is this match forbid?"

"Fatal fault!" exclaimed the *rishi*, "fault that wipeth all his grace,
Fault, that human power nor effort, rite nor penance can efface!

Fatal fault or destined sorrow! for it is decreed on high,
On this day, a twelve-month later, this ill-fated prince will die!"

Shook the startled king in terror, and in fear and trembling cried:
"Unto short-lived, fated bridegroom ne'er my child shall be allied!

Come, Savitri, dear-loved maiden! choose another happier lord,
Rishi Narad speaketh wisdom, list unto his holy word!

Every grace and every virtue, is effaced by cruel Fate,
On this day a twelve-month later, leaves the prince his mortal state!"

"Father!" answered thus the maiden, soft and sad her accents fell,
"I have heard thy honoured mandate, holy Narad counsels well,

Pardon witless maiden's feelings! but beneath the eye of Heaven,
Only once a maiden chooseth, twice her troth may not be given!

Long his life or be it narrow, and his virtues great or none,
Brave Satyavan is my husband, he my heart and troth hath won!

What a maiden's heart hath chosen that a maiden's lips confess,
True to him, thy poor Savitri goes into the wilderness!"

"Monarch!" uttered then the *rishi*, "fixed is she in mind and heart,
From her troth the true Savitri never, never will depart!

More than mortal's share of virtue hath been to Satyavan given,
Let the true maid wed her chosen, leave the rest to gracious Heaven!"

"*Rishi* and preceptor holy!" so the weeping monarch prayed,
"Heaven avert all future evils, and thy mandate is obeyed!"

Narad wished him joy and gladness, blessed the loving youth and maid,
Forest hermits on their wedding every fervent blessing laid.

IV

Overtaken by Fate

Twelve-month in the darksome forest by her true and chosen lord,
Lived Savitri, served his parents by her thought and deed and word,

Bark of tree supplied her garments draped upon her bosom fair,
Or the red cloth as in *asrams* holy women love to wear,

And the aged queen she tended with a fond and filial pride,
Served the old and sightless monarch like a daughter by his side,

And with love and gentle sweetness pleased her husband and her lord,
But in secret, night and morning, pondered still on Narad's word!

Nearer came the fatal morning by the holy Narad told,
Fair Savitri reckoned daily and her heart was still and cold,

Three short days remaining only! and she took a vow severe
Of *triratra*, three nights' penance, holy fasts and vigils drear!

Of Savitri's rigid penance heard the king with anxious woe,
Spake to her in loving accents, so the vow she might forego:

"Hard the penance, gentle daughter, and thy woman's limbs are frail,
After three nights' fasts and vigils sure thy tender health may fail!"

"Be not anxious, loving father," meekly thus Savitri prayed,
"Penance I have undertaken, will unto the gods be made!"

Much misdoubting then the monarch gave his sad and slow assent,
Pale with fast and unseen tear-drops, lonesome nights Savitri spent.

Nearer came the fatal morning, and to-morrow he shall die!
Dark, dark hours of nightly silence! Tearless, sleepless is her eye!

"Dawns that dread and fated morning!" said Savitri, bloodless, brave,
Prayed her fervent prayers in silence, to the Fire oblations gave,

Bowed unto the forest Brahmans, to the parents kind and good,
Joined her hands in salutation and in reverent silence stood.

With the usual morning blessing, "*Widow may'st thou never be,*"
Anchorites and agéd Brahmans blessed Savitri fervently,

O! that blessing fell upon her like the rain on thirsty air,
Struggling hope inspired her bosom as she drank those accents fair!

But returned the dark remembrance of the *rishi* Narad's word,
Pale she watched the creeping sunbeams, mused upon her fated lord!

"Daughter, now thy fast is over," so the loving parents said,
"Take thy diet after penance, for thy morning prayers are prayed,"

"Pardon, father," said Savitri, "let this other day be done,"
Unshed tear-drops filled her eyelids, glistened in the morning sun!

Young Satyavan, tall and stately, ponderous axe on shoulder hung,
For the distant darksome jungle issued forth serene and strong,

But unto him came Savitri, and in sweetest accents prayed,
As upon his manly bosom gently she her forehead laid:

"Long I wished to see the jungle where steals not the solar ray,
Take me to the darksome forest, husband! let me go to-day!"

"Come not, love," Satyavan answered with a loving husband's care,
"Thou art all unused to labour, forest paths thou may'st not dare,

And with recent fasts and vigils pale and bloodless is thy face,
And thy steps are weak and feeble, jungle paths thou may'st not trace."

"Fasts and vigils make me stronger," said the wife with wifely pride,
"Toil I shall not feel nor languor, when my lord is by my side,

For I feel a woman's longing with my lord to trace the way,
Grant me, husband ever gracious, with thee let me go to-day!"

Answered then the loving husband, as his hands in hers he wove,
'Ask permission from my parents in the trackless woods to rove."

Then Savitri to the monarch, urged her longing, strange request,
After duteous salutation thus her humble prayer addrest:

"To the jungle goes my husband, fuel and the fruit to seek,
I would follow if my mother and my loving father speak,

Twelve-month from this narrow *asram* hath Savitri stepped nor strayed,
In this cottage true and faithful ever hath Savitri stayed,

For the sacrificial fuel wends my lord his lonesome way,
Please my kind and loving parents, I would follow him to-day."

"Never since her wedding morning," so the loving king replied,
"Wish or thought Savitri whispered, for a boon or object sighed,

Daughter, thy request is granted, safely in the forest roam,
Safely with thy lord and husband, seek again thy cottage home."

Bowing to her loving parents did the fair Savitri part,
Smile upon her pallid features, anguish in her inmost heart!

Round her sylvan greenwoods blossomed 'neath a cloudless Indian sky,
Flocks of pea-fowls gorgeous plumaged flew before her wondering eye,

Woodland rills and crystal nullahs gently rolled o'er rocky bed,
Flower-decked hills in dewy brightness towering glittered overhead,

Birds of song and beauteous feather trilled a note in every grove,
Sweeter accents fell upon her, from her husband's lips of love!

Still with thoughtful eye Savitri watched her dear and fated lord,
Flail of grief was in her bosom, but her pale lips shaped no word,

And she listened to her husband, still on anxious thought intent,
Cleft in two her throbbing bosom, as in silence still she went!

Gaily with the gathered wild-fruits did the prince his basket fill,
Hew the interlacéd branches with his might and practised skill,

Till the drops stood on his forehead, weary was his aching head,
Faint he came unto Savitri, and in faltering accents said:

"Cruel ache is on my forehead, fond and ever faithful wife,
And I feel a hundred needles pierce me and torment my life,

And my feeble footsteps falter, and my senses seem to reel,
Fair would I beside thee linger, for a sleep doth o'er me steal."

With a wild and speechless terror pale Savitri held her lord,
On her lap his head she rested and she laid him on the sward,

सावित्री सत्यवांश्च ।

Savitri and Satyavean.

Narad's fatal words remembered as she watched her husband's head,
Burning lip and pallid forehead, and the dark and creeping shade,

Clasped him in her beating bosom, kissed his lips with panting breath,
Darker grew the lonesome forest, and he slept the sleep of death!

V

Triumph over Fate

In the bosom of the shadows rose a Vision dark and dread,
Shape of gloom in inky garment, and a crown was on his head!

Gleaming form of sable splendour, blood-red was his sparkling eye,
And a fatal noose he carried, grim and godlike, dark and high!

And he stood in solemn silence, looked in silence on the dead,
And Savitri on the greensward gently placed her husband's head,

And a tremor shook Savitri, but a woman's love is strong,
With her hands upon her bosom thus she spake with quivering tongue:

"More than mortal is thy glory, and a radiant god thou be!
Tell me what bright name thou bearest, and thy message unto me."

"Know me," thus responded YAMA, "mighty monarch of the dead,
"Mortals leaving earthly mansion to my darksome realms are led,

Since with woman's full affection thou hast loved thy husband dear,
Hence before thee, faithful woman, YAMA doth in form appear,

But his days and loves are ended, and he leaves his faithful wife,
In this noose I bind and carry spark of his immortal life,

Virtue graced his life and action, spotless was his princely heart,
Hence for him I came in person, princess, let thy husband part."

YAMA from Satyavan's body, pale and bloodless, cold and dumb,
Drew the vital spark, *purusha*, smaller than the human thumb,

In his noose the spark he fastened, silent went his darksome way,
Left the body shorn of lustre to its rigid cold decay.

Southward went the dark-hued YAMA with the youth's immortal life,
And, for her woman's love abideth, followed still the faithful wife.

"Turn Savitri," outspake YAMA, "for thy husband loved and lost,
Do the rites due unto mortals by their Fate predestined crost,

For thy wifely duty ceases, follow not in fruitless woe,
And no farther living creature may with monarch YAMA go!"

"But I may not chose but follow where thou takest my husband's life,
For Eternal Law divides not loving man and faithful wife!

For my love and my affection, for a woman's sacred woe,
Grant me in thy godlike mercy farther still with him I go!

Fourfold are our human duties: first, to study holy lore;
Then to live as good householders, feed the hungry at our door;

Then to pass our days in penance; last to fix our thoughts above;
But the final goal of virtue, it is Truth and deathless Love!"

"True and holy are thy precepts," listening YAMA made reply,
"And they fill my heart with gladness and with pious purpose high,

I would bless thee, fair Savitri, but the dead come not to life,
Ask for other boon and blessing, faithful, true and virtuous wife!"

"Since you so permit me, YAMA," so the good Savitri said,
"For my husband's banished father let my dearest suit be made,

Sightless in the darksome forest dwells the monarch faint and weak,
Grant him sight and grant him vigour, YAMA, in thy mercy speak!"

"Duteous daughter!" YAMA answered, "be thy pious wishes given,
And his eyes shall be restoréd to the cheerful light of heaven,

Turn, Savitri, faint and weary, follow not in fruitless woe,
And no farther living creature may with monarch YAMA go!"

"Faint nor weary is Savitri," so the noble princess said,
"Since she waits upon her husband, gracious Monarch of the dead,

What befalls the wedded husband still befalls the faithful wife,
Where he goes she ever follows, be it death or be it life!

And our sacred writ ordaineth and our pious *rishis* sing,
Transient meeting with the holy doth its countless blessings bring,

Longer friendship with the holy purifies the mortal birth,
Lasting union with the holy is the bright sky on the earth!

Union with the pure and holy is immortal heavenly life,
For Eternal Law divides not loving man and faithful wife!"

"Blesséd are thy words," said Yama, "blesséd is thy pious thought,
With a higher purer wisdom are thy holy lessons fraught,

I would bless thee, fair Savitri, but the dead come not to life,
Ask for other boon and blessing, faithful, true and virtuous wife!"

"Since you so permit me, Yama," so the good Savitri said,
"Once more for my husband's father be my supplication made,

Lost his kingdom, in the forest dwells the monarch faint and weak,
Grant him back his wealth and kingdom, Yama, in thy mercy speak!"

"Loving daughter!" Yama answered, "on him I this boon bestow,
Turn, Savitri, living mortal may not with King Yama go!"

Still Savitri, meek and faithful, followed her departed lord,
Yama still with higher wisdom listened to her saintly word,

And the Sable King was vanquished, and he turned on her again,
And his words fell on Savitri like the cooling summer rain!

"Noble woman, speak thy wishes, name thy boon and purpose high,
What the pious mortal asketh gods in heaven may not deny!"

"Thou hast," so Savitri answered, "granted father's realm and might,
To his vain and sightless eyeballs hast restored their blesséd sight,

Grant him that the line of monarchs may not all untimely end,
That his kingdom to Satyavan's and Savitri's sons descend!"

"Have thy object," answered YAMA, "and thy lord shall live again,
He shall live to be a father, and your children too shall reign,

For a woman's troth abideth longer than the fleeting breath,
And a woman's love abideth, higher than the doom of Death!"

VI

Return Home

Vanished then the Sable Monarch, and Savitri held her way
Where in dense and darksome forest still her husband lifeless lay,

And she sat upon the greensward by the cold unconscious dead,
On her lap with deeper kindness placed Satyavan's lifeless head,

And that touch of true affection thrilled him back to waking life,
As returned from distant regions gazed the prince upon his wife!

"Have I lain too long and slumbered, sweet Savitri, faithful spouse?
But I dreamt a Sable Person, in a noose took forth my life!"

"Pillowed on this lap," she answered, "long upon the earth you lay,
And the Sable Person, husband, he hath come and passed away,

Rise and leave this darksome forest if thou feelest light and strong,
For the night is on the jungle and our way is dark and long."

Rising as from happy slumber looked Satyavan on all around,
Saw the wide-extending jungle mantling all the darksome ground,

"Yes," he said, "I now remember, ever loving faithful dame,
We in search of fruit and fuel to this lonesome forest came.

As I hewed the gnarléd branches, cruel anguish filled my brain,
And I laid me on the greensward with a throbbing piercing pain,

Pillowed on thy gentle bosom, solaced by thy gentle love,
I was soothed, and drowsy slumber fell on me from skies above.

All was dark, and then I witnessed, was it but a fleeting dream,
God or Vision, dark and dreadful, in the deepening shadows gleam!

Was this dream my fair Savitri, dost thou of this Vision know?
Tell me, for before my eyesight still the Vision seems to glow!"

"Darkness thickens," said Savitri, "and the evening waxeth late,
When the morrow's light returneth I shall all these scenes narrate,

Now arise, for darkness gathers, deeper grows the gloomy night,
And thy loving anxious parents trembling wait thy welcome sight.

Hark the rangers of the forest! how their voices strike the ear!
Prowlers of the darksome jungle! how they fill my breast with fear!

Forest-fire is raging yonder, for I see a distant gleam,
And the rising evening breezes help the red and radiant beam,

Let me fetch a burning faggot and prepare a friendly light,
With these fallen withered branches chase the shadows of the night,

And if feeble still thy footsteps,—long and weary is our way,—
By the fire repose, my husband, and return by light of day."

"For my parents, fondly anxious," thus Satyavan made reply,
"Pains my heart and yearns my bosom, let us to their cottage hie,

When I tarried in the jungle or by day or dewy eve,
Searching in the hermitages often did my parents grieve,

And with father's soft reproaches and with mother's loving fears,
Chid me for my tardy footsteps, dewed me with their gentle tears!

Think then of my father's sorrow, of my mother's woeful plight,
If afar in wood and jungle pass we now the livelong night,

Wife beloved, I may not fathom what mishap or load of care,
Unknown dangers, unseen sorrows even now my parents share!"

Gentle drops of filial sorrow trickled down his manly eye,
Fond Savitri sweetly speaking softly wiped the tear-drops dry:

"Trust me, husband, if Savitri hath been faithful in her love,
If she hath with pious offerings served the righteous gods above,

If she hath a sister's kindness unto brother men performed,
If she hath in speech and action unto holy truth conformed,

Unknown blessings, mighty gladness, trust thy ever faithful wife,
And not sorrows or disasters wait this eve our parents' life!"

Then she rose and tied her tresses, gently helped her lord to rise,
Walked with him the pathless jungle, looked with love into his eyes,

On her neck his clasping left arm sweetly winds in soft embrace,
Round his waist Savitri's right arm doth as sweetly interlace,

Thus they walked the darksome jungle, silent stars looked from above,
And the hushed and throbbing midnight watched Savitri's deathless love!

BOOK VI

GO-HARANA

(Cattle-Lifting)

THE conditions of the banishment of the sons of Pandu were hard. They must pass twelve years in exile, and then they must remain a year in concealment. If they were discovered within this last year, they must go into exile for another twelve years.

Having passed the twelve years of exile in forests, the Pandav brothers disguised themselves and entered into the menial service of Virata, king of the Matsyas, to pass the year of concealment. Yudhishthir presented himself as a Brahman, skilled in dice, and became a courtier of the king. Bhima entered the king's service as cook. For Arjun, who was so well known, a stricter concealment was necessary. He wore conch bangles and earrings and braided his hair, like those unfortunate beings whom nature has debarred from the privileges of men and women, and he lived in the inner apartments of the king. He assumed the name of *Brihannala,* and taught the inmates of the royal household in music and dancing. Nakula became a keeper of the king's horses, and Sahadeva took charge of the king's cows. Draupadi too disguised herself as a waiting-woman, and served the princess of the Matsya house in that humble capacity.

In these disguises the Pandav brothers safely passed a year in concealment in spite of all search which Duryodhan made after them. At last an incident happened which led to their discovery when the year was out.

Cattle-lifting was a common practice with the kings of ancient India, as with the chiefs of ancient Greece. The king of the Trigartas and the king of the Kurus combined and fell on the king of the Matsyas in order to drive off the numerous herd of fine cattle for which his kingdom was famed. The Trigartas entered the Matsya kingdom from the south-east, and while Virata went out with his troops to meet the foe, Duryodhan with his Kuru forces fell on the kingdom from the north.

When news came that the Kurus had invaded the kingdom, there was no army in the capital to defend it. King Virata had gone out with most of his troops to face the Trigartas in the south-east, and the prince Uttara had no inclination to face the Kurus in the north. The disguised Arjun now came to the rescue in the manner described in this Book. The description of the bows, arrows, and swords of the Pandav brothers which they had concealed in a tree, wrapped like human corpses to frighten inquisitive travellers, throws some light on the arts and manufactures of ancient times. The portions translated in this Book form Sections xxxv., xxxvi., xl. to xliii., a portion of Section xliv., and Sections liii. and lxxii. of Book iv. of the original text.

I

Complaint of the Cowherd

Monarch of the mighty Matsyas, brave Virata known to fame,
Marched against Trigarta chieftains who from southward regions came,

From the north the proud Duryodhan, stealing onwards day by day,
Swooped on Matsya's fattened cattle like the hawk upon its prey!

Bhishma, Drona, peerless Karna, led the Kuru warriors brave,
Swept the kingdom of Virata like the ocean's surging wave,

Fell upon the trembling cowherds, chased them from the pasture-field,
Sixty thousand head of cattle was the Matsya country's yield!

And the wailing chief of cowherds fled forlorn, fatigued and spent,
Speeding on his rapid chariot to the royal city went,

Came inside the city portals, came within the palace gate,
Struck his forehead in his anguish, and bewailed his luckless fate.

Meeting there the prince Uttara, youth of beauty and of fame,
Told him of the Kurus' outrage and lamented Matsya's shame:

"Sixty thousand head of cattle, bred of Matsya's finest breed,
To Hastina's distant empire do the Kuru chieftains lead!

Glory of the Matsya nation! save thy father's valued kine,
Quick thy footsteps, strong thy valour, vengeance deep and dire be
thine!

'Gainst the fierce Trigarta chieftains Matsya's warlike king is gone,
Thee we count our lord and saviour as our monarch's gallant son!

Rise, Uttara! beat the Kurus, homeward lead the stolen kine,
Like an elephant in the jungle, pierce the Kurus' shattered line!

As the *Vina* speaketh music, by musicians tuned aright,
Let thy sounding bow and arrows speak thy deeds of matchless might!

Harness quick thy milk-white coursers to thy sounding battle-car,
Hoist thy goldeo lion-banner, speed thee, prince, unto the war!

And as thunder-wielding INDRA smote *asuras* fierce and bold,
Smite the Kurus with thy arrows winged with plumes of yellow gold!

As the famed and warlike Arjun is the stay of Kuru's race,
Thou art refuge of the Matsyas and thy kingdom's pride and grace!"

But the prince went not to battle from the foe to guard the State,
To the cowherd answered gaily, sheltered by the palace gate!

"Not unknown to me the usage of the bow and wingéd dart,
Not unknown the warrior's duty or the warrior's noble art,

I would win my father's cattle from the wily foeman's greed,
If a skilful chariot-driver could my fiery coursers lead,

For my ancient chariot-driver died on battle's gory plain,
Eight and twenty days we wrestled, many warlike chiefs were slain!

Bring me forth a skilful driver who can urge the battle-steed,
I will hoist my lion-banner, to the dubious hattle speed!

Dashing through the foeman's horses, ranks of elephant and car,
I will win the stolen cattle rescued in the field of war!

And like thunder-wielding INDRA, smiting Danu's sons of old,
I will smite the Kuru chieftians, drive them to their distant hold!

Bhishma and the proud Duryodan, archer Karna known to fame,
Drona too shall quail before me and retreat in bitter shame!

Do those warriors in my absence Matsya's far-famed cattle steal?
But beneath my countless arrows Matsya's vengeance they shall feel!

Bring me forth a chariot-driver, let me speed my battle-car,
And in wonder they will question—Is this Arjun famed in war?"

II

The Disguised Charioteer

Arjun, guised as Brihannala, heard the boast Uttara made,
And to try his skill and valour, thus to fair Draupadi prayed:

"Say to him that Brihannala will his battle-chariot lead,
That as Arjun's chariot-driver he hath learned to urge the steed,

Say that faithful Brihannala many a dubious war hath seen,
And will win his father's cattle in this contest fierce and keen."

Fair Draupadi, guised as menial, Arjun's secret hest obeyed,
Humbly stepped before Uttara and in gentle accents prayed:

"Hear me, prince! yon Brihannala will thy battle-chariot lead,
He was Arjun's chariot-driver, skilled to urge the flying steed,

Trained in war by mighty Arjun, trained to drive the battle-car,
He hath followed helméd Arjun in the glorious field of war,

And when Arjun conquered Khandav, this, Uttara, I have seen,
Brihannala drove his chariot, for I served Yudhishthir's queen."

Heard Uttara hesitating, spake his faint and timid mind,
"I would trust thee, beauteous maiden, lotus-bosomed, ever kind!

But a poor and sexless creature, can he rein the warlike steed?
Can I ask him, worse than woman, in the battle's ranks to lead?"

"Need is none," Draupadi answered, "Brihannala's grace to ask,
He is eager like the war-horse for this great and warlike task!

And he waits upon thy sister, she will bid the minion speed,
And he wins thy father's cattle, and the victor's glorious meed!"

Matsya's princess spake to Arjun, Arjun led the battle-car,
Led the doubting prince Uttara to the dread and dubious war!

III

Arms and Weapons

Arjun drove the prince of Matsya to a darksome *sami* tree,
Spake unto the timid warrior in his accents bold and free:

"Prince, thy bow and shining arrows, pretty handsome toys are these,
Scarcely they beseem a warrior, and a warrior cannot please!

Thou shalt find upon this *sami*, mark my words which never fail,
Stately bows and wingéd arrows, banners, swords and coats of mail!

And a bow which strongest warriors scarce can in the battle bend,
And the limits of a kingdom widen when that bow is strained!

Tall and slender like a palm-tree, worthy of a warrior bold,
Smooth the wood of hardened fibre, and the ends are yellow gold!"

Doubting still Uttara answered: "In this *sami's* gloomy shade
Corpses hang since many seasons, in their wrappings duly laid,

Now I mark them all suspended, horrent, in the open air,
And to touch the unclean objects, friend, is more than I can dare!"

"Fear not warrior," Arjun answered, "for the tree conceals no dead,
Warriors' weapons, cased like corpses, lurk within its gloomy shade,

And I ask thee, prince of Matsya, not to touch an unclean thing,
But unto a chief and warrior weapons and his arms to bring!"

Prince Uttara gently lighted, climbed the dark and leafy tree,
Arjun from the prince's chariot bade him speed the arms to free,

Then the young prince cut the wrappings and the shining bows appear,
Twisted, voiced like hissing serpents, like the bright stars glistening clear!

Seized with wonder prince Uttara silently the weapons eyed,
And unto his chariot-driver thus in trembling accents cried:

"Whose this bow so tall and stately, speak to me my gentle friend,
On the wood are golden bosses, tipped with gold at either end?

Whose this second ponderous weapon, stout and massive in the hold,
On the staff are worked by artists elephants of burnished gold?

Sure some great and mighty monarch owns this other bow of might,
Set with golden glittering insects on its ebon back so bright?

Golden suns of wondrous brightness on this fourth their lustre lend,
Who may be the unknown archer who this stately bow can bend?

And the fifth is set with jewels, gems and stones of purest ray,
Golden fire-flies glint and sparkle in the yellow light of day!

Who doth own these shining arrows with their heads in gold encased,
Thousand arrows bright and feathered, in the golden quivers placed?

Next are these with vulture-feather, golden-yellow in their hue,
Made of iron, keen and whetted, whose may be these arrows true?

Next upon this sable quiver jungle tigers worked in gold,
And these keen and boar-eared arrows speak some chieftain fierce and bold!

Uttara and Arjun discovering the arms.

Fourth are these seven hundred arrows, crescent is their shining blade,
Thirsting for the blood of foemen, and by cunning artists made!

And the fifth are golden-crested, made of tempered steel and bright,
Parrot feathers wing these arrows, whetted and of wondrous might!

Who doth own this wondrous sabre, shape of toad is on the hilt,
On the blade a toad is graven, and the scabbard nobly gilt?

Larger, stouter is this second in its sheath of tiger-skin,
Decked with bells and gold-surmounted, and the blade is bright and
keen!

Next this scimitar so curious, by the skilled *nishadas* made,
Scabbard made of wondrous cowhide sheathes the bright and polished
blade!

Fourth, a long and beauteous weapon, glittering sable in its hüe,
With its sheath of softer goat-skin, worked with gold on azure blue!

And the fifth is broad and massive, over thirty fingers long,
Golden-sheathed, and gold embosséd, like a snake or fiery tongue!"

Joyously responded Arjun: "Mark this bow embossed with gold,
'Tis the wondrous bow, *gandiva*, worthy of a warrior bold!

Gift of heaven! to archer Arjun kindly gods this weapon sent,
And the confines of a kingdom widen when the bow is bent!

Next, this mighty ponderous weapon worked with elephants of gold,
With this bow the stalwart Bhima hath the tide of conquests rolled!

And the third with golden insects with a cunning hand inlaid,
'Tis Yudhishthir's royal weapon by the noblest artists made!

Next the bow with solar lustre brave Nakula wields in fight,
And the fifth is Sahadeva's, decked with gems and jewels bright!

Listen, prince! these thousand arrows, unto Arjun they belong,
And the darts whose blades are crescent unto Bhima brave and strong,

Boar-ear shafts are young Nakula's, in the tiger-quiver cased,
Sahadeva owns the arrows with the parrot's feather graced,

These three-knotted, shining arrows, thick and yellow vulture-plumed,
They belong to King Yudhishthir, with their heads by gold illumed.

Listen more! if of these sabres, prince of Matsya, thou wouldst know,
Arjun's sword is toad-engraven, ever dreaded by the foe!

And the sword in tiger-scabbard, massive and of mighty strength,
None save tiger-waisted Bhima wields that sword of wondrous length!

Next the sabre golden-hilted, sable and with gold embossed,
Brave Yudhishthir kept that sabre when the king his kingdom lost!

Yonder sword with goat-skin scabbard brave Nakula wields in war,
In the cowhide Sahadeva keeps his shining scimitar!"

"Strange thy accents," spake Uttara, "stranger are these weapons bright,
Are they arms of sons of Pandu famed on earth for matchless might?

Where are now those pious princes by a dire misfortune crossed,
Warlike Arjun, good Yudhishthir, by his subjects loved and lost?

Where is tiger-waisted Bhima, matchless fighter in the field,
And the brave and twin-born brothers skilled the arms of war to wield?

O'er a game they lost their empire, and we heard of them no more,
Or perchance they lonesome wander on some wild and distant shore!

And Draupadi, noble princess, purest, best of womankind,
Doth she wander with Yudhishthir, changeless in her heart and mind?"

Proudly answered valiant Arjun, and a smile was on his face,
"Not in distant lands the brothers do their wandering footsteps trace!

In thy father's court disguiséd lives Yudhishthir just and good,
Bhima in thy father's palace as a cook prepares the food!

Brave Nakula guards the horses, Sahadeva tends the kine,
As thy sister's waiting-woman doth the fair Draupadi shine!

Pardon, prince, these rings and bangles, pardon strange unmanly guise,
'Tis no poor and sexless creature, Arjun greets thy wondering eyes!"

IV

Rescue of the Cattle

Arjun decked his mighty stature in the gleaming arms of war,
And with voice of distant thunder rolled the mighty battle-car!

And the Kurus marked with wonder Arjun's standard lifted proud,
Heard with dread the deep *gandiva* sounding oft and sounding loud!

And they knew the wondrous bowman wheeling round the battle-car,
And with doubts and grave misgivings whispered Drona skilled in war:

"That is Arjun's monkey-standard, how it greets my ancient eyes!
Well the Kurus know the standard like a comet in the skies!

Hear ye not the deep *gandiva?* How my ear its accents greet!
Mark ye not these pointed arrows falling prone before my feet?

By these darts his salutation to his teacher loved of old,
Years of exile now completed, Arjun sends with greetings bold!

How the gallant prince advances! Now I mark his form and face,
Issuing from his dark concealment with a brighter, haughtier grace!

Well I know his bow and arrows and I know his standard well,
And the deep and echoing accents of his far-resounding shell!

In his shining arms accoutred, gleaming in his helmet dread,
Shines he like the flame of *homa*, by libations duly fed!"

Arjun marked the Kuru warriors arming for th' impending war,
Whispered thus to prince Uttara as he drove the battle-car:

"Stop thy steeds, O prince of Matsya! for too close we may not go,
Stop thy chariot whence my arrows reach and slay the distant foe,

Seek we out the Kuru monarch, proud Duryodhan let us meet,
If he falls we win the battle, other chieftains will retreat.

There is Drona, my preceptor, Drona's warlike son is there,
Kripa and the mighty Bhishma, archer Karna, tall and fair,

Them I seek not in this battle, lead, O lead thy chariot far,
Midst the chiefs Duryodhan moves not, moves not in the ranks of war!

But to save the pilfered cattle speeds he onward in his fear,
While these warriors stay and tarry to defend their monarch's rear,

But I leave these car-borne warriors, other work to-day is mine,
Meet Duryodhan in the battle, win thy father's stolen kine!"

Matsya's prince then turned the coursers, left behind the war's array,
Where Duryodhan with the cattle quickly held his onward way,

Kripa marked the course of Arjun, guessed his inmost thought aright,
Thus he spake to brother warriors urging speed and instant fight:

"Mark ye, chieftains, gallant Arjun wheels his sounding battle-car,
'Gainst our prince the proud Duryodhan seeks to turn the tide of war!

Let us fall upon our foeman and our prince and leader save,
Few save INDRA, god of battles, conquers Arjun fierce and brave!

What were Matsya's fattened cattle, many thousands though they be,
If our monarch sinks in battle like a ship in stormy sea!"

Vain were Kripa's words of wisdom! Arjun drove the chariot fair,
While his shafts like countless locusts whistled through the ambient air!

Kuru soldiers struck with panic neither stood and fought, nor fled,
Gazed upon the distant Arjun, gazed upon their comrades dead!

Arjun twanged his mighty weapon, blew his far-resounding shell,
Strangely spake his monkey-standard, Kuru warriors knew it well!

Sankha's voice, *gandiva's* accents, and the chariot's booming sound,
Filled the air like distant thunder, shook the firm and solid ground!

Kuru soldiers fled in terror, or they slumbered with the dead,
And the rescued lowing cattle, with their tails uplifted, fled!

V

Warrior's Guerdon

Now with joy the king Virata to his royal city came,
Saw the rescued herds of cattle, saw Uttara prince of fame,

Marked with wonder gallant Arjun, helmet-wearing, armour-cased,
Knew Yudhishthir and his brothers, now as royal princes dressed,

And he greeted good Yudhishthir, truth-beloving, brave and strong,
And to valiant Arjun offered Matsya's princess fair and young!

"Pardon, monarch," answered Arjun, "but I may not take as bride,
Matsya's young and beauteous princess whom I love with father's
pride!

She hath often met me trusting in the inner palace hall,
As a daughter on a father waited on my loving call,

I have trained her *kokil* accents, taught her maiden steps in dance,
Watched her skill and varied graces all her native charms enhance!

Pure is she in thought and action, spotless as my hero boy,
Grant her to my son, O monarch, as his wedded wife and joy!

Abhimanyu trained in battle, handsome youth of godlike face,
Krishna's sister, fair Subhadra, bore the child of princely grace!

Worthy of thy youthful daughter, pure in heart and undefiled,
Grant it, sire! my Abhimanyu wed thy young and beauteous child!"

Answered Matsya's noble monarch with a glad and grateful heart:
"Words like these befit thy virtue, nobly hast thou done thy part!

Be it as thou sayest, Arjun; unto Pandu's race allied,
Matsya's royal line is honoured, Matsya's king is gratified!"

VI

The Wedding

Good Yudhishthir heard the tidings, and he gave his free assent,
Unto distant chiefs and monarchs kindly invitations sent,

In the town of Upa-plavya, of fair Matsya's towns the best,
Made their home the pious brothers to receive each royal guest.

Came unto them Kasi's monarch and his arméd troopers came,
And the king of fair Panchala with his sons of warlike fame,

Came the sons of fair Draupadi, early trained in art of war,
Other chiefs and sacrificers came from regions near and far.

Krishna decked in floral garlands with his elder brother came,
And his sister fair Subhadra, Arjun's loved and longing dame,

Arjun's son brave Abhimanyu came upon his flowery car,
And with elephants and chargers, troopers trained in art of war.

Vrishnis from the sea-girt Dwarka, brave Andhakas known to fame,
Bhojas from the mighty Chumbal with the righteous Krishna came,

He to gallant sons of Pandu made his presents rich and rare,
Gems and gold and costly garments, slaves and damsels passing fair.

With its quaint and festive greetings came at last the bridal day,
Matsya maids were merry-hearted and the Pandav brothers gay!

Conch and cymbal, horn and trumpet spake forth music soft and sweet,
In Virata's royal palace, in the peopled mart and street!

And they slayed the jungle red-deer, and they spread the ample board,
And prepared the cooling palm-drink, and the richest viands stored!

Mimes and actors please the people, bards recite the ancient song,
Glories of heroic houses minstrels by their lays prolong!

And deep-bosomed dames of Matsya, jasmin-form and lotus-face,
With their pearls and golden garlands joyously the bridal grace!

Circled by those royal ladies, though they all are bright and fair,
Brightest shines the fair Draupadi with a beauty rich and rare!

Stately dames and merry maidens lead the young and soft-eyed bride,
As the queens of gods encircle INDRA's daughter in her pride!

Arjun from the Matsya monarch takes the princess passing fair,
For his son by fair Subhadra, nursed by Krishna's loving care,

With a godlike grace Yudhishthir stands by faithful Arjun's side,
As a father takes a daughter, takes the young and beauteous bride,

Joins her hand to Abhimanyu's, and with cake and parchéd rice,
On the altar brightly blazing doth the holy sacrifice.

Matsya's monarch on the bridegroom rich and costly presents pressed,
Elephants he gave two hundred, steeds seven thousand of the best,

Poured libations on the altar, on the priests bestowed his gold,
Offered to the sons of Pandu rich domain and wealth untold!

With a pious hand Yudhishthir, true in heart and pure in mind,
Made his gifts in gold and garments, kine and wealth of every kind,

Costly chariots, beds of splendour, robes with thread of gold belaced,
Viands rich and sweet confection, drinks the richest and the best,

Lands he gave unto the Brahman, bullocks to the labouring swain,
Steeds he gave unto the warrior, to the people gifts and grain,

And the city of the Matsyas, teeming with a wealth untold,
Shone with festive joy and gladness and with flags and cloth of gold!

BOOK VII

UDYOGA

(The Preparation)

THE term of banishment having expired, Yudhishthir demanded that the kingdom of Indra-prastha should be restored to him. The old Dhrita-rashtra and his queen and the aged and virtuous councillors advised the restoration, but the jealous Duryodhan hated his cousins with a genuine hatred, and would not consent. All negotiations were therefore futile, and preparations were made on both sides for the most sanguinary and disastrous battle that had ever been witnessed in Northern India.

The portions translated in this Book are from Sections i., ii., ii., xciv., cxxiv., and cxxvi. of Book v. of the original text.

I

Krishna's Speech

Mirth and song and nuptial music waked the echoes of the night,
Youthful bosoms throbbed with pleasure, love-lit glances sparkled bright,

But when young and white-robed USHAS ope'd the golden gates of day,
To Virata's council chamber chieftains thoughtful held their way.

Stones inlaid in arch and pillar glinted in the glittering dawn,
Gay festoons and graceful garlands o'er the golden cushions shone!

Matsya's king, Panchala's monarch, foremost seats of honour claim,
Krishna too and Valadeva, Dwarka's chiefs of righteous fame!

By them sate the bold Satyaki from the sea-girt western shore,
And the godlike sons of Pandu,—days of dark concealment o'er!

Youthful princes in their splendour graced Virata's royal hall,
Valiant sons of valiant fathers, brave in war, august and tall!

In their gem-bespangled garments came the warriors proud and high,
Till the council chamber glittered like the star-bespangled sky!

Kind the greetings, sweet the converse, soft the golden moments fly,
Till intent on graver questions all on Krishna turn their eye,

Krishna with his inner vision then the state of things surveyed,
And his thoughts before the monarchs thus in weighty accents laid:

"Known to all, ye mighty monarchs! May your glory ever last!
True to plighted word Yudhishthir hath his weary exile passed,

Twelve long years with fair Draupadi in the pathless jungle strayed,
And a year in menial service in Virata's palace stayed,

He hath kept his plighted promise, braved affliction, woe and shame,
And he begs, assembled monarchs, ye shall now his duty name!

For he swerveth not from duty kingdom of the sky to win,
Prizeth hamlet more than empire, so his course be free from sin,

Loss of realm and wealth and glory higher virtues in him prove,
Thoughts of peace and not of anger still the good Yudhishthir move!

Mark again the sleepless anger and the unrelenting hate
Harboured by the proud Duryodhan driven by his luckless fate,

From a child, by fire or poison, impious guile or trick of dice,
He hath compassed dark destruction, by deceit and low device!

Ponder well, ye gracious monarchs, with a just and righteous mind,
Help Yudhishthir with your counsel, with your grace and blessings
kind,

Should the noble son of Pandu seek his right by open war,
Seek the aid of righteous monarchs and of chieftains near and far?

Should he smite his ancient foemen skilled in each deceitful art,
Unforgiving in their vengeance, unrelenting in their heart?

Should he rather send a message to the proud unbending foe,
And Duryodhan's haughty purpose seek by messenger to know?

Should he send a noble envoy, trained in virtue, true and wise,
With his greetings to Duryodhan in a meek and friendly guise?

Ask him to restore the kingdom on the sacred Jumna's shore?
Either king may rule his empire as in happy days of yore!"

Krishna uttered words of wisdom pregnant with his peaceful thought,
For in peace and not by bloodshed still Yudhishthir's right he sought.

II

Valadeva's Speech

Krishna's elder Valadeva, stalwart chief who bore the plough,
Rose and spake, the blood of Vrishnis mantled o'er his lofty brow:

"Ye have listened, pious monarchs, to my brother's gentle word
Love he bears to good Yudhishthir and to proud Hastina's lord,

For his realm by dark blue Jumna good Yudhishthir held of yore,
Brave Duryodhan ruled his kingdom on the ruddy Ganga's shore,

And once more in love and friendship either prince may rule his share,
For the lands are broad and fertile, and each realm is rich and fair!

Speed the envoy to Hastina with our love and greetings kind,
Let him speak Yudhishthir's wishes, seek to know Duryodhan's mind,

Make obeisance unto Bhishma and to Drona true and bold,
Unto Kripa, archer Karna, unto chieftains young and old,

To the sons of Dhrita-rashtra, rulers of the Kuru land,
Righteous in their kingly duties, stout of heart and strong of hand,

To these princes and to burghers gathered in the council hall,
Let him speak Yudhishthir's wishes, plead Yudhishthir's cause to all.

Speak he not in futile anger, for Duryodhan holds the power,
And Yudhishthir's wrath were folly in this sad and luckless hour!

By his dearest friends dissauded, but by rage or madness driven,
He hath played and lost his empire, may his folly be forgiven!

Indra-prastha's spacious empire now Duryodhan deems his own,
By his tears and soft entreaty let Yudhishthir seek the throne!

Open war I do not counsel, humbly seek Duryodhan's grace,
War will not restore the empire nor the gambler's loss replace!"

Thus with cold and cruel candour stalwart Valadeva cried,
Wrathful rose the brave Satyaki, fiercely thus to him replied:

III

Satyaki's Speech

"Shame unto the halting chieftain who thus pleads Duryodhan's part,
Timid counsel, Valadeva, speaks a woman's timid heart!

Oft from warlike stock ariseth weakling chief who bends the knee,
As a withered branch and fruitless springeth from a fruitful tree!

From a heart so faint and craven, faint and craven words must flow,
Monarchs in their pride and glory list not to such counsel low!

Could'st thou, impious Valadeva, midst these potentates of fame,
On Yudhishthir pious-hearted cast this undeservéd blame?

Challenged by his wily foeman, and by dark misfortune crost,
Trusting to their faith Yudhishthir played a righteous game and lost!

Challenge from a crownéd monarch can a crownéd king decline,
Can a Kshatra warrior fathom fraud in sons of royal line?

Nathless he surrendered empire true to faith and plighted word,
Lived for years in pathless forests Indra-prastha's mighty lord!

Past his years of weary exile, now demands his realm of old,
Claims it, not as humble suppliant, but as king and warrior bold!

Past his year of dark concealment, bold Yudhishthir claims his own,
Proud Duryodhan now must render Indra-prastha's jewelled throne!

Bhishma counsels, Drona urges, Kripa pleads for right in vain,
False Duryodhan will not render sinful conquest, fraudful gain!

Open war I therefore counsel, ruthless and relentless war,
Grace we seek not when we meet them speeding in our battle-car!

And our weapons, not entreaties, shall our foemen force to yield,
Yield Yudhishthir's rightful kingdom or they perish on the field!

False Duryodhan and his forces fall beneath our battle's shock,
As beneath the bolt of thunder falls the crushed and riven rock!

Who shall meet the helméd Arjun in the gory field of war,
Krishna with his fiery discus mounted on his battle-car?

Who shall face the twin-born brothers by the mighty Bhima led,
And the vengeful chief Satyaki with his bow and arrows dread?

Ancient Drupad wields his weapon peerless in the field of fight,
And his brave son, born of AGNI, owns an all-consuming might!

Abhimanyu, son of Arjun, whom the fair Subhadra bore,
And whose happy nuptials brought us from far Dwarka's sea-girt shore,

Men on earth nor bright immortals can the youthful hero face,
When with more than Arjun's prowess Abhimanyu leads the race!

Dhrita-rashtra's sons we conquer and Gandhara's wily son,
Vanquish Karna though world-honoured for his deeds of valour done,

Win the fierce-contested battle and redeem Yudhishthir's own,
Place the exile pious-hearted on his father's ancient throne!

And no sin Satyaki reckons slaughter of the mortal foe,
But to beg a grace of foemen were a mortal sin and woe!

Speed we then unto our duty, let our impious foemen yield,
Or the fiery son of Sini meets them on the battle-field!"

IV

Drupad's Speech

Fair Panchala's ancient monarch rose his secret thoughts to tell,
From his lips the words of wisdom with a graceful accent fell:

"Much I fear thou speakest truly, hard is Kuru's stubborn race,
Vain the hope, the effort futile, to beseech Duryodhan's grace!

Dhrita-rashtra pleadeth vainly, feeble is his fitful star,
Ancient Bhishma, righteous Drona, cannot stop this fatal war,

Archer Karna thirsts for battle, moved by jealousy and pride,
Deep Sakuni, false and wily, still supports Duryodhan's side!

Vain is Valadeva's counsel, vainly shall our envoy plead,
Half his empire proud Duryodhan yields not in his boundless greed,

In his pride he deems our mildness faint and feeble-hearted fear,
And our suit will fan his glory and his arrogance will cheer!

Therefore let our many heralds travel near and travel far,
Seek alliance of all monarchs in the great impending war,

Unto brave and noble chieftains, unto nations east and west,
North and south to warlike races speed our message and request!

Meanwhile peace and offered friendship we before Duryodhan place,
And my priest will seek Hastina, strive to win Duryodhan's grace,

If he renders Indra-prastha, peace will crown the happy land,
Or our troops will shake the empire from the east to western strand!"

Vainly were Panchala's Brahmans sent with messages of peace,
Vainly urged Hastina's elders that the fatal feud should cease,

Proud Duryodhan to his kinsmen would not yield their proper share,
Pandu's sons would not surrender, for they had the will to dare!

Fatal war and dire destruction do the mighty gods ordain,
Till the kings and arméd nations strew the red and reeking plain!

Krishna in his righteous effort sought for wisdom from above,
Strove to stop the war of nations and to end the feud in love!

And to far Hastina's palace Krishna went to sue for peace,
Raised his voice against the slaughter, begged that strife and feud
should cease!

V

Krishna's Speech at Hastina

Silent sat the listening chieftains in Hastina's council hall,
With the voice of rolling thunder Krishna spake unto them all:

"Listen, mighty Dhrita-rashtra, Kuru's great and ancient king,
Seek not war and death of kinsmen, word of peace and love I bring!

'Midst the wide earth's many nations Bharats in their worth excel,
Love and kindness, spotless virtue, in the Kuru-elders dwell,

Father of that noble nation, now retired from life's turmoil,
Ill beseems that sin or untruth should thy ancient bosom soil!

For thy sons in impious anger seek to do their kinsmen wrong,
And withhold the throne and kingdom which by right to them belong,

And a danger thus ariseth like the comet's baleful fire,
Slaughtered kinsmen, bleeding nations, soon shall feed its fatal ire!

Stretch thy hands, O Kuru monarch! prove thy truth and holy grace,
Man of peace! avert the slaughter, and preserve thy ancient race,

Yet restrain thy fiery children, for thy mandates they obey,
I with sweet and soft persuasion Pandu's truthful sons will sway.

'Tis thy profit, Kuru monarch! that the fatal feud should cease,
Brave Duryodhan, good Yudhishthir, rule in unmolested peace,

Pandu's sons are strong in valour, mighty is their arméd hand,
INDRA shall not shake thy empire when they guard the Kuru land!

Bhishma is thy kingdom's bulwark, doughty Drona rules the war,
Karna matchless with his arrows, Kripa peerless in his car,

Let Yudhishthir and stout Bhima by these noble warriors stand,
And let helmet-wearing Arjun guard the sacred Kuru land,

Who shall then contest thy prowess from the sea to farthest sea,
Ruler of a world-wide empire, king of kings and nations free?

Sons and grandsons, friends and kinsmen will surround thee in a ring,
And a race of loving heroes guard their ancient hero-king!

Dhrita-rashtra's lofty edicts will proclaim his boundless sway,
Nations work his righteous mandates and the kings his will obey!

If this concord be rejected, and the lust of war prevail,
Soon within these ancient chambers will resound the sound of wail!

Grant thy children be victorious and the sons of Pandu slain,
Dear to thee are Pandu's children, sure their death must cause thee pain!

But the Pandavs, skilled in warfare, are renowned both near and far,
And thy race and children's slaughter will methinks pollute this war,

Sons and grandsons, loving princes, thou shalt never see again,
Kinsmen loved and car-borne chieftains will bedeck the gory plain!

Ponder yet, O ancient monarch! Rulers of each distant State,
Nations from the farthest regions gather thick to court their fate,

Father of a righteous nation! Save the princes of the land,
On the armed and fated nations stretch, old man, thy saving hand!

Say the word! and at thy bidding leaders of each hostile race
Not the gory field of battle, but the festive board will grace,

Robed in jewels, decked in garlands, they will quaff the ruddy wine,
Greet their foes in mutual kindness, bless thy holy name and thine!

Think, O man of many seasons! When good Pandu left this throne,
And his helpless loving orphans thou didst cherish as thine own,

'Twas thy helping steadying fingers taught their infant steps to frame,
'Twas thy loving gentle accents taught their lips to lisp each name,

As thine own they grew and blossomed, dear to thee they yet remain,
Take them back unto thy bosom, be a father once again!

Unto thee, O Dhrita-rashtra! Pandu's sons in homage bend,
And a loving peaceful message through my willing lips they send:

Tell our monarch, more than father, by his sacred sweet command
We have lived in pathless jungle, wandered far from land to land,

True unto our plighted promise, for we ever felt and knew,
To his promise Dhrita-rashtra cannot, will not be untrue!

Years of anxious toil are over and of woe and bitterness,
Years of waiting and of watching, years of danger and distress,

Like a dark unending midnight hung on us this age forlorn,
Streaks of hope and dawning brightness usher now the radiant morn!

Be unto us as a father, loving, not inspired by wrath,
Be unto us as preceptor, pointing us the righteous path,

If perchance astray we wander, thy strong arm shall lead aright,
If our feeble bosom fainteth, help us with a father's might!

This O king! the soft entreaty Pandu's sons to thee have made,
These are words the sons of Pandu through me unto thee have said,

Take their love, O gracious monarch! Let thy closing days be fair,
Let Duryodhan keep his kingdom, let the Pandavs have their share.

Call to mind their noble suffering, for the tale is dark and long
Of the outrage they have suffered, of the insult and the wrong!

Exiled into Varnavata, destined unto death by flame,
For the gods assist the righteous, they with added prowess came!

Exiled unto Indra-prastha, by their toil and by their might
Cleared a forest, built a city, did the *rajasuya* rite!

Cheated of their realm and empire and of all they called their own,
In the jungle they have wandered, and in Matsya lived unknown,

Once more quelling every evil they are stout of heart and hand,
Now redeem thy plighted promise, and restore their throne and land!

Trust me, mighty Dhrita-rashtra! trust me, lords who grace this hall,
Krishna pleads for peace and virtue, blessings unto you and all!

Slaughter not the arméd nations, slaughter not thy kith and kin,
Mark not, king, thy closing winters with the bloody stain of sin!

Pandu's sons and thy own children, let them guard thy ancient throne,
Cherish peace and cherish virtue, for thy days are almost done!"

VI

Bhishma's Speech

From the monarch's ancient bosom sighs and sobs convulsive broke,
Bhishma wiped his manly eyelids and to proud Duryodhan spoke:

"Listen, prince! for righteous Krishna counsels love and holy peace,
Listen, youth! and may thy fortune with thy passing years increase!

Yield to Krishna's words of wisdom, for thy weal he nobly strives,
Yield and save thy friends and kinsmen, save thy cherished subjects' lives!

Foremost race in all this wide earth is Hastina's royal line,
Bring not on them dire destruction by a sinful act of thine!

Sons and fathers, friends and brothers, shall in mutual conflict die,
Kinsmen slain by dearest kinsmen shall upon the red field lie!

Hearken unto Krishna's counsel, unto wise Vidura's word,
Be thy mother's fond entreaty and thy father's mandate heard!

Tempt not *devas'* fiery vengeance on thy old heroic race,
Tread not in the path of darkness, seek the path of light and grace!

Listen to thy king and father, he hath Kuru's empire graced,
Listen to thy queen and mother, she who nursed thee on her breast!"

VII

Drona's Speech

Out spake Drona, priest and warrior, and his words were few and high,
Clouded was Duryodhan's forehead, wrathful was Duryodhan's eye:

"Thou hast heard the holy counsel which the righteous Krishna said,
Ancient Bhishma's voice of warning thou hast in thy bosom weighed,

Peerless in their godlike wisdom are these chiefs in peace or strife,
Truest friends to thee, Duryodhan, pure and sinless in their life,

Take their counsel, and thy kinsmen fasten in the bonds of peace,
May the empire of the Kurus and their warlike fame increase!

List unto thy old preceptor! Faithless is thy fitful star,
False they feed with hopes thy bosom, those who urge and counsel war!

Crownéd kings and arméd nations, they will strive for thee in vain,
Vainly brothers, sons, and kinsmen will for thee their life-blood drain,

For the victor's crown and glory never, never can be thine,
Krishna conquers, and brave Arjun! mark these deathless words of mine!

I have trained the youthful Arjun, seen him bend the warlike bow,
Marked him charge the hostile forces, marked him smite the scattered foe!

Fiery son of Jamadagni owned no greater, loftier might,
Breathes on earth no mortal warrior conquers Arjun in the fight!

Krishna too, in war resistless, comes from Dwarka's distant shore,
And the bright-gods quake before him whom the fair Devaki bore!

These are foes thou may'st not conquer, take an ancient warrior's word,
Act thou as thy heart decideth, thou art Kuru's king and lord!"

VIII

Vidura's Speech

Then in gentler voice Vidura sought his pensive mind to tell,
From his lips serene and softly words of woe and anguish fell:

"Not for thee I grieve, Duryodhan, slain by vengeance fierce and keen,
For thy father weeps my bosom, and the aged Kuru queen!

Sons and grandsons, friends and kinsmen slaughtered in this fatal war,
Homeless, cheerless, on this wide earth they shall wander long and far!

Friendless, kinless, on this wide earth whither shall they turn and fly?
Like some bird bereft of plumage, they shall pine awhile and die!

Of their race the sad survivors, they shall wander o'er the earth,
Curse the fatal day, Duryodhan, saw thy sad and woeful birth."

IX

Dhrita-rashtra's Speech

Tear-drops filled his sightless eyeballs, anguish shook his aged frame,
As the monarch soothed Duryodhan by each fond endearing name:

"Listen, dearest son, Duryodhan, shun this dark and fatal strife,
Cast not grief and death's black shadow on thy parents' closing life!

Krishna's heart is pure and spotless, true and wise the words he said,
We may win a world-wide empire with the noble Krishna's aid!

Seek the friendship of Yudhishthir, loved of righteous gods above,
And unite the scattered Kurus by the lasting tie of love!

Now at full is tide of fortune, never may it come again,
Strive and win! or ever after all repentance may be vain!

Peace is righteous Krishna's counsel, and he offers loving peace,
Take the offered boon, Duryodhan! Let all strife and hatred cease!"

X

Duryodhan's Speech

Silent sat the proud Duryodhan, wrathful in the council hall,
Spake to mighty-armèd Krishna, and to Kuru warriors all:

"Ill becomes thee, Dwarka's chieftain, in the paths of sin to move,
Bear for me a secret hatred, for the Pandavs secret love!

And my father, wise Vidura, Bhishma, Drona warrior bold,
Join thee in this bitter hatred, turn on me their glances cold!

What great crime or darkening sorrow shadows o'er my bitter fate,
That ye chiefs and Kuru's monarch mark Duryodhan for your hate?

Speak, what nameless guilt or folly, secret sin to me unknown,
Turns from me your sweet affection, father's love that was my own?

If Yudhishthir, fond of gambling, played a heedless, reckless game,
Lost his empire and his freedom, was it then Duryodhan's blame?

And if freed from shame and bondage in his folly played again,
Lost again and went to exile, wherefore doth he now complain?

Weak are they in friends and forces, feeble is their fitful star,
Wherefore then in pride and folly seek with us unequal war?

Shall we, who to mighty INDRA scarce will do the homage due,
Bow to homeless sons of Pandu and their comrades faint and few?

Bow to them while warlike Drona leads us as in days of old,
Bhishma greater than the bright-gods, archer Karna true and bold?

If in dubious game of battle we should forfeit fame and life,
Heaven will ope its golden portals for the Kshatras slain in strife!

If unbending to our foemen we should press the gory plain,
Stingless is the bed of arrows, death for us will have no pain!

For the Kshatra knows no terror of his foeman in the field,
Breaks like hardened forest timber, bends not, knows not how to yield!

So the ancient sage Matanga of the warlike Kshatra said,
Save to priest and sage preceptor unto none he bends his head!

Indra-prastha which my father weakly to Yudhishthir gave,
Nevermore shall go unto him while I live and brothers brave!

Kuru's undivided kingdom Dhrita-rashtra rules alone,
Let us sheathe our swords in friendship and the monarch's empire own!

If in past in thoughtless folly once the realm was broke in twain,
Kuru-land is re-united, never shall be split again!

Take my message to my kinsmen, for Duryodhan's words are plain,
Portion of the Kuru empire sons of Pandu seek in vain!

Town nor village, mart nor hamlet, help us righteous gods in heaven,
Spot that needle's point can cover shall not unto them be given!"

BOOK VIII

BHISHMA-BADHA

(Fall of Bhishma)

ALL negotiations for a peaceful partition of the Kuru kingdom having failed, both parties now prepared for a battle, perhaps the most sanguinary that was fought on the plains of India in the ancient times. It was a battle of nations, for all the warlike races in Northern India took a share in it.

Duryodhan's army consisted of his own division, as well as the divisions of ten allied kings. Each allied power is said to have brought one *akshauhini* troops, and if we reduce this fabulous number to the moderate figure of ten thousand, including horse and foot, cars and elephants, Duryodhan's army including his own division was over a hundred thousand strong.

Yudhishthir had a smaller army, said to have been seven *akshauhinis* in number, which we may, by a similar reduction, reckon to be seventy thousand. His father-in-law, the king of the Panchalas, and Arjun's relative, the king of the Matsyas, were his principal allies. Krishna joined him as his friend and adviser, and as the charioteer of Arjun, but the Vrishnis as a nation had joined Duryodhan.

When the two armies were drawn up in array and faced each other, and Arjun saw his revered elders and dear friends and relations among his foes, he was unwilling to fight. It was on this occasion that Krishna explained to him the great principles of Duty in that memorable work called the *Bhagavat-gita* which has been translated into several European languages. Belief in one Supreme Deity is the underlying thought of this work, and ever and anon, as Professor Garbe remarks, "does Krishna revert to the doctrine that for every man, no matter to what caste he may belong, the zealous performance of his duty and the discharge of his obligations is his most important work."

Duryodhan chose the grand old fighter Bhishma as the commander-in-chief of his army, and for ten days Bhishma held his own and inflicted serious loss on Yudhishthir's army. The principal incidents of these ten days, ending with the fall of Bhishma, are narrated in this Book.

This Book is an abridgment of Book vi. of the original text.

I

Pandavs routed by Bhishma

USHAS with her crimson fingers oped the portals of the day,
Nations armed for mortal combat in the field of battle lay!

Beat of drum and blare of trumpet and the *sankha's* lofty sound,
By the answering cloud repeated, shook the hills and tented ground,

And the voice of sounding weapons which the warlike archers drew,
And the neigh of battle chargers as the arméd horsemen flew,

Mingled with the rolling thunder of each swiftly-speeding car,
And with pealing bells proclaiming mighty elephants of war!

Bhishma led the Kuru forces, strong as Death's resistless flail,
Human chiefs nor bright Immortals could against his might prevail,

Helmet-wearing, gallant Arjun came in pride and mighty wrath,
Held aloft his famed *gandiva*, strove to cross the chieftain's path!

Abhimanyu, son of Arjun, whom the fair Subhadra bore,
Drove against Kosala's monarch famed in arms and holy lore,

Hurling down Kosala's standard he the dubious combat won,
Barely escaped with life the monarch from the fiery Arjun's son!

With his fated foe Duryodhan, Bhima strove in deathful war,
And against the proud Duhsasan brave Nakula drove his car,

Sahadeva, mighty bowman, then the fierce Durmukha sought,
And the righteous king Yudhishthir with the car-borne Salya fought,

Ancient feud and deathless hatred fired the Brahman warrior bold,
Drona with the proud Panchalas fought once more his feud of old!

Nations from the Eastern regions 'gainst the bold Virata pressed,
Kripa met the wild Kaikeyas hailing from the furthest West,

Drupad, proud and peerless monarch, with his cohorts onward bore
'Gainst the warlike Jayadratha, chief of Sindhu's sounding shore,

Chedis and the valiant Matsyas, nations gathered from afar,
Bhojas and the fierce Kambojas mingled in the dubious war!

Through the day the battle lasted, and no mortal tongue can tell
What unnumbered chieftains perished and what countless soldiers fell,

And the son knew not his father, and the sire knew not his son,
Brother fought against his brother, strange the deeds of valour done!

Horses fell, and shafts of chariots shivered in resistless shock,
Hurled against the foeman's chariots, speeding like the rolling rock,

Elephants by *mahuts* driven furiously each other tore,
Trumpeting with trunks uplifted, on the serried soldiers bore!

Ceaseless plied the gallant troopers, with a stern unyielding might,
Pikes and axes, clubs and maces, swords and spears and lances bright,

Horsemen flew as forkéd lightning, heroes fought in shining mail,
Archers poured their feathered arrows like the bright and glistening
hail!

Bhishma, leader of the Kurus, as declined the dreadful day,
Through the shattered Pandav legions forced his all-resistless way,

Onward went his palm-tree standard through the hostile ranks of war,
Matsyas, Kasis, nor Panchalas faced the mighty Bhishma's car!

But the fiery son of Arjun, filled with shame and bitter wrath,
Turned his car and tawny coursers to obstruct the chieftain's path,

Vainly fought the youthful warrior, though his darts were pointed well,
And dissevered from his chariot Bhishma's palm-tree standard fell,

Anger stirred the ancient Bhishma, and he rose in all his might,
Abhimanyu, pierced with arrows, fell and fainted in the fight!

Then to save the son of Arjun, Matsya's gallant princes came,
Brave Uttara, noble Sweta, youthful warriors known to fame,

Ah! too early fell the warriors in that sad and fatal strife,
Matsya's dames and dark-eyed maidens wept the princes' shortened
life!

Slain by cruel fate, untimely, two brave princes young and good,
Dauntless still the youngest brother, proud and gallant Sankha stood!

But the helmet-wearing Arjun came to stop the victor's path,
And to save the fearless Sankha from the ancient Bhishma's wrath,

Drupad too, Panchala's monarch, swiftly rushed into the fray,
Strove to shield the broken Pandavs and to stop the victor's way,

But as fire consumes the forest, wrathful Bhishma slew the foe,
None could face his sounding chariot and his ever-circled bow!

And the fainting Pandav warriors marked the foe, resistless, bold,
Shook like unprotected cattle tethered in the blighting cold!

Onward came the mighty Bhishma, and the slaughter fiercer grew,
From his bow like hissing serpents still the glistening arrows flew!

Onward came the ancient warrior, and his path was strewn with dead,
And the broken Pandav forces, crushed and driven, scattered fled!

Friendly night and gathering darkness closed the slaughter of the day,
To their tents the sons of Pandu held their sad and weary way!

II

Kurus routed by Arjun

Grieved at heart the good Yudhishthir wept the losses of the day,
Sought the aid of gallant Krishna for the morning's fresh array,

And when from the eastern mountains SURYA drove his fiery car,
Krishna and the helméd Arjun strove to turn the tide of war!

Bhishma's glorious palm-tree standard o'er the field of battle rose,
Arjun's monkey standard glittered, cleaving through the serried foes,

Devas from their cloud-borne chariots, and *gandharvas* from the sky,
Gazed in mute and speechless wonder on the human chiefs from high!

While with dauntless valour Arjun still the mighty Bhishma sought,
Warlike prince of fair Panchala with the doughty Drona fought,

Ceaseless 'gainst the proud preceptor sent his darts like summer rain,
Baffled by the skill of Drona, Dhrista-dyumna strove in vain!

But the fiercer darts of Drona pierced the prince's shattered mail,
Hurtling on his battle chariot like an angry shower of hail,

And they rent in twain his bowstring, and they cut his pond'rous mace,
Slew his steeds and chariot-driver, streaked with blood his godlike face!

Dauntless still, Panchala's hero, springing from his shattered car,
Like a hungry desert lion with his sabre rushed to war,

Dashed aside the darts of Drona with his broad and ample shield,
With his sabre brightly flaming fearless trod the reddened field!

In his fury and his rashness he had fallen on that day,
But the ever-watchful Bhima stopped the proud preceptor's way!

Proud Duryodhan marked with anger Bhima rushing in his car,
And he sent Kalinga's forces to the thickening ranks of war,

Onward came Kalinga warriors with the dark tornado's might,
Dusky chiefs, Nishada warriors, gloomy as the sable night!

Rose the shout of warring nations surging to the battle's fore,
Like the angry voice of tempest and the ocean's troubled roar!

And like darkly rolling breakers ranks of serried warriors flew,
Scarcely in the thickening darkness friends and kin from foemen knew!

Fell the young prince of Kalinga by the wrathful Bhima slain,
But against Kalinga's monarch baffled Bhima fought in vain,

Safely sat the eastern monarch on his *howda's* lofty seat,
Till upon the giant tusker Bhima sprang with agile feet,

Then he struck with fatal fury, brave Kalinga fell in twain,
Scattered fled his countless forces, when they saw their leader slain!

Darkly rolled the tide of battle where Duryodhan's valiant son
Strove against the son of Arjun famed for deeds of valour done,

Proud Duryodhan marked the contest with a father's anxious heart,
Came to save his gallant Lakshman from brave Abhimanyu's dart,

And the helmet-wearing Arjun marked his son among his foes,
Wheeled from far his battle-chariot and in wrath terrific rose!

"Arjun!" "Arjun!" cried the Kurus, and in panic broke and fled,
Steed and tusker turned from battle, soldiers fell among the dead!

Godlike Krishna drove the coursers of resistless Arjun's car,
And the sound of Arjun's *sankha* rose above the cry of war!

And the voice of his *gandiva* spread a terror far and near,
Crushed and broken, faint and frightened, fled the Kurus in their fear!

Onward still through scattered foemen conquering Arjun held his way,
Till the evening's gathering darkness closed the action of the day!

III

Bhishma and Arjun meet

Anxious was the proud Duryodhan when the golden morning came,
For before the car of Arjun fled each Kuru chief of fame,

Brave Duryodhan shook in anger, and a tremor moved his frame,
As he spake to ancient Bhishma words of wrath in bitter shame:

"Bhishma! dost thou lead the Kurus in this battle's crimson field?
Warlike Drona, doth he guard us like a broad and ample shield?

Wherefore then before yon Arjun do the valiant Kurus fly?
Wherefore doth our leader linger when he hears the battle cry?

Doth a secret love for Pandavs quell our leader's matchless might?
With a halting zeal for Kurus doth the noble Bhishma fight?

Pardon, chief! if for the Pandavs doth thy partial heart incline,
Yield thy place! let faithful Karna lead my gallant Kuru line!"

Anger flamed on Bhishma's forehead and the tear was in his eye,
And in accents few and trembling thus the warrior made reply:

"Vain our toil, unwise Duryodhan! Nor can Bhishma warrior old,
Nor can Drona skilled in weapons, Karna archer proud and bold,

Wash the stain of deeds unholy and of wrongs and outraged laws,
Conquer with a load of cunning 'gainst a right and righteous cause!

Deaf to wisdom's voice, Duryodhan! deaf to parents and to kin,
Thou shalt perish in thy folly, in thy unrepented sin!

For the wrongs and insults offered unto good Yudhishthir's wife,
For the kingdom from him stolen, for the plots against his life,

For the dreadful oath of Bhima, for the holy counsel given,
Vainly given by saintly Krishna, thou art doomed by righteous Heaven!

Meanwhile since he leads thy forces, Bhishma still shall meet his foe,
Or to conquer, or to perish, to the battle's front I go."

Speaking thus, unto the battle ancient Bhishma held his way,
Sweeping all before his chariot as upon a previous day,

And the army of Yudhishthir shook from end to farthest end,
Arjun nor the valiant Krishna could against the tide contend!

Cars were shattered, fled the coursers, elephants were pierced and slain,
Shafts of chariots, broken standards, lifeless soldiers strewed the plain!

Coats of mail were left by warriors as they ran with streaming hair,
Soldiers fled like herds of cattle stricken by a sudden fear!

Krishna, Arjun's chariot-driver, and a chief of righteous fame,
Marked the Pandav's broken forces, spake in grief and bitter shame:

"Arjun! not in hour of battle hath it been thy wont to fly,
Forward lay thy path of glory, or to conquer or to die!

If to-day with angry Bhishma Arjun shuns the dubious fight,
Shame on Khrishna! if he joins thee in this sad inglorious flight!

Be it mine alone, O Arjun! warrior's wonted work to know,
Krishna with his fiery discus smites the all-resistless foe!"

Then he flung the reins to Arjun, left the steeds and sounding car,
Leaped upon the field of battle, rushed into the dreadful war!

"Shame!" cried Arjun in his anger, "Krishna shall not wage the fight,
Nor shall Arjun like a recreant seek for safety in his flight!"

And he dashed behind the warrior, and on foot the chief pursued,
Caught him as the angry Krishna still his distant foeman viewed,

Stalwart Arjun lifted Krishna, as the storm lifts up a tree,
Placed him on his battle-chariot, and he bent to him his knee:

"Pardon, Krishna, this compulsion! pardon this transgression bold,
But while Arjun lives, O chieftain! weapon of thy wrath withhold!

By my warlike Abhimanyu, fair Subhadra's darling boy,
By my brothers, dearer, truer, than in hours of pride and joy,

By my troth I pledge thee, Krishna,—let thy angry discus sleep,—
Archer Arjun meets his foeman, and his plighted word will keep."

Forthwith rushed the fiery Arjun in his sounding battle-car,
And like waves before him parted serried ranks of hostile war,

Vainly hurled his lance Duryodhan 'gainst the valiant warrior's face,
Vainly Salya, king of Madra, threw with skill his pond'rous mace,

With disdain the godlike Arjun dashed the feeble darts aside,
Held aloft his famed *gandiva*, as he stood with haughty pride,

Beat of drum and blare of *sankha* and the thunder of his car,
And his weapon's fearful accents rose terrific near and far!

Came resistless Pandav forces, sweeping onward, wave on wave,
Chedis, Matsyas and Panchalas, chieftians true and warriors brave!

Onward too came forth the Kurus, by the matchless Bhishma led,
Shouts arose and cry of anguish midst the dying and the dead!

But the evening closed in darkness, and the night-fires fitful flared,
Fainting troops and bleeding chieftains to their various tents repaired!

IV

Duryodhan's Brothers slain

Dawned another day of battle; Kurus knew that day too well,
Widowed queens of fair Hastina wept before the evening fell!

For as whirlwind of destruction Bhima swept in mighty wrath,
Broke the serried line of tuskers vainly sent to cross his path,

Smote Duryodhan with his arrows, three terrific darts and five,
Smote proud Salya; from the battle scarce they bore the chiefs alive!

Krishna and Arjun driving towards Bhishma.

Then Duryodhan's fourteen brothers rushed into the dreadful fray,
Fatal was the luckless moment, inauspicious was the day!

Licked his mouth the vengeful Bhima, and he shook his bow and lance,
As the lion lolls his red tongue when he sees his prey advance!

Short and fierce the furious combat; six pale princes turned and fled,
Eight of proud Duryodhan's brothers fell and slumbered with the dead!

V

Satyaki's Sons slain

Morning with her fiery radiance oped the portals of the day,
Shone once more on Kuru warriors, Pandav chiefs in dread array!

Bhima and the gallant Arjun led once more the van of war,
But the proud preceptor Drona faced them in his sounding car!

Still with gallant son of Arjun, Lakshman strove with bow and shield,
Vainly strove; his faithful henchman bore him bleeding from the field!

Lakshman, son of proud Duryodhan! Abhimanyu, Arjun's son!
Doomed to die in youth and glory 'neath the same revolving sun!

Sad the day for Vrishni warriors! Brave Satyaki's sons of might,
'Gainst the cruel Bhuri-sravas strove in unrelenting fight,

Ten brave brothers, pride of Vrishni, fell upon that fatal day,
Slain by mighty Bhuri-sravas, and upon the red field lay!

VI

Bhima's Danger and Rescue

Dawned another day of slaughter; heedless Bhima forced his way,
Through Duryodhan's serried legions, where dark death and danger
lay,

And a hundred foeman gathered, and unequal was the strife,
Bhima strove with furious valour, for his forfeit was his life!

Fair Panchala's watchful monarch saw the danger from afar,
Forced his way where bleeding Bhima fought beside his shattered car,

And he helped the fainting warrior, placed him on his chariot-seat,
But the Kurus darkly gathered, surging round as waters meet!

Arjun's son and twelve brave chieftains dashed into the dubious fray,
Rescued Bhima and proud Drupad from the Kurus' grim array,

Surging still the Kuru forces onward came with ceaseless might,
Drona smote the scattered Pandavs till the darksome hours of night!

VII

Pandavs routed by Bhishma

Morning came and angry Arjun rushed into the dreadful war,
Krishna drove his milk-white coursers, onward flew his sounding car,

And before his monkey banner quailed the faint and frightened foes,
Till like star on billowy ocean Bhishma's palm-tree banner rose!

Vainly then the good Yudhishthir, stalwart Bhima, Arjun brave,
Strove with useless toil and valour shattered ranks of war to save,

Vainly too the Pandav brothers on the peerless Bhishma fell,
Gods in sky nor earthly warriors Bhishma's matchless might could quell!

Fell Yudhishthir's lofty standard, shook his chariot, battle-tost,
Fell his proud and fiery coursers, and the dreadful day was lost!

Sahadeva and Nakula vainly strove with all their might,
Till their broken scattered forces rested in the shades of night!

VIII

Iravat slain: Duryodhan's Brothers slain

Morning saw the turn of battle; Bhishma's charioteer was slain,
And his coursers uncontrolléd flew across the reddened plain,

Ill it fared with Kuru forces when their leader went astray,
And their foremost chiefs and warriors with the dead and dying lay.

But Gandhara's mounted princes rode across the battle-ground,—
For its steeds and matchless chargers is Gandhara's realm renowned,

And to smite the young Iravat fierce Gandhara's princes swore,—
Brave Iravat, son of Arjun, whom a Naga princess bore!

Mounted on their milk-white chargers proudly did the princes sweep,
Like the sea-birds skimming gaily o'er the bosom of the deep,

Five of stout Gandhara's princes in that fatal combat fell,
And a sixth in fear and faintness fled to tell the woeful tale!

Short, alas! Iravat's triumph, transient was the victor's joy,
Alambusha dark and dreadful came against the gallant boy,

Fierce and fateful was the combat, mournful is the tale to tell,
Like a lotus rudely severed, gallant son of Arjun fell!

Arjun heard the tale of sorrow, and his heart was filled with grief,
Thus he spake a father's anguish, faint his accents, few and brief:

"Wherefore, Krishna, for a kingdom mingle in this fatal fray?
Kinsmen killed and children slaughtered,—dear, alas! the price
we pay!

Woe unto Hastina's empire built upon our kinsmen's grave!
Dearer than the throne of monarchs was Iravat young and brave!

Young in years and rich in beauty, with thy mother's winsome eye!
Art thou slain, my gallant warrior, and thy father was not nigh?

But thy young blood calls for vengeance! noble Krishna drive the car,
Let them feel the father's prowess, those who slew the son in war!"

And he dashed the glistening tear-drop, and his words were few and brief,
Broken ranks and slaughtered chieftains spoke an angry father's grief!

Bhima too revenged Iravat, and as onward still he flew,
Brothers of the proud Duryodhan in that fatal combat slew!

Still advanced the fatal carnage till the darksome close of day,
When the wounded and the weary with the dead and dying lay!

IX

Pandavs routed by Bhishma

Fell the thickening shades of darkness on the red and ghastly plain,
Torches by the white tents flickered, red fires showed the countless slain,

With a bosom sorrow-laden proud Duryodhan drew his breath,
Wept the issue of the battle and his warlike brothers' death.

Spent with grief and silent sorrow slow the Kuru monarch went
Where arose in dewy starlight Bhishma's proud and snowy tent,

And with tears and hands conjoinéd thus the sad Duryodhan spoke,
And his mournful bitter accents oft by heaving sighs were broke:

"Bhishma! on thy matchless prowess Kuru's hopes and fates depend,
Gods nor men with warlike Bhishma can in field of war contend!

Brave in war are sons of Pandu, but they face not Bhishma's might,
In their fierce and deathless hatred slay my brothers in the fight!

Mind thy pledge, O chief of Kurus, save Hastina's royal race,
On the ancient king my father grant thy never-failing grace!

If within thy noble bosom,—pardon cruel words I say,—
Secret love for sons of Pandu holds a soft and partial sway,

If thy inner heart's affections unto Pandu's sons incline,
Grant that Karna lead my forces 'gainst the foeman's hostile line!"

Bhishma's heart was full of sadness and his eyelids dropped a tear,
Soft and mournful were his accents and his vision true and clear:

"Vain, Duryodhan, is this contest, and thy mighty host is vain,
Why with blood of friendly nations drench this red and reeking plain?

They must win who, strong in virtue, fight for virtue's stainless laws,
Doubly armed the stalwart warrior who is armed in righteous cause!

Think, Duryodhan, when *gandharvas* took thee captive and a slave,
Did not Arjun rend thy fetters, Arjun righteous chief and brave?

When in Matsya's fields of pasture captured we Virata's kine,
Did not Arjun in his valour beat thy countless force and mine?

Krishna now hath come to Arjun, Krishna drives his battle-car,
Gods nor men can face these heroes in the field of righteous war!

Ruin frowns on thee, Duryodhan, and upon thy impious State,
In thy pride and in thy folly thou hast courted cruel fate!

Bhishma still will do his duty, and his end it is not far,
Then may other chieftains follow,—fatal is this Kuru war!"

Dawned a day of mighty slaughter and of dread and deathful war,
Ancient Bhishma in his anger drove once more his sounding car!

Morn to noon and noon to evening none could face the victor's wrath,
Broke and shattered, faint and frightened, Pandavs fled before his path!

Still amidst the dead and dying moved his proud resistless car,
Till the gathering night and darkness closed the horrors of the war!

X

Fall of Bhishma

Good Yudhishthir gazed with sorrow on the dark and ghastly plain,
Shed his tears on chiefs and warriors by the matchless Bhishma slain!

"Vain this unavailing battle, vain this woeful loss of life,
'Gainst the death-compelling Bhishma hopeless is this arduous strife!

As a lordly tusker tramples on a marsh of feeble reeds,
As a forest conflagration on the parchéd woodland feeds,

Bhishma rides upon my warriors in his mighty battle-car,
God nor mortal chief can face him in the gory field of war!

Vain our toil, and vain the valour of our kinsmen loved and lost,
Vainly fight my faithful brothers by a luckless fortune crost,

Nations pour their life-blood vainly, ceaseless wakes the sound of woe,
Krishna, stop this cruel carnage, unto woods once more we go!"

Sad they hold a midnight council and the chiefs in silence meet,
And they go to ancient Bhishma, love and mercy to entreat,

Bhishma loved the sons of Pandu with a father's loving heart,
But from troth unto Duryodhan righteous Bhishma would not part!

"Sons of Pandu!" said the chieftain, "Prince Duryodhan is my lord,
Bhishma is no faithless servant nor will break his plighted word,

Valiant are ye, noble princes, but the chief is yet unborn,
While I lead the course of battle, who the tide of war can turn!

Listen more. With vanquished foeman, or who falls or takes to flight,
Casts his weapons, craves for mercy, ancient Bhishma doth not fight,

Bhishma doth not fight a rival who submits, fatigued and worn,
Bhishma doth not fight the wounded, doth not fight a woman born."

Back unto their tents the Pandavs came with Krishna deep and wise,
He unto the anxious Arjun thus in solemn whisper cries:

"Arjun, there is hope of triumph! Hath not truthful Bhishma sworn,
He will fight no wounded warrior, he will fight no woman born?

Female child was brave Sikhandin, Drupad's youngest son of pride,
Gods have turned him to a warrior, placed him by Yudhishthir's side!

Place him in the van of battle, mighty Bhishma leaves the strife,
Then with ease we fight and conquer, and the forfeit is his life!"

"Shame!" exclaimed the angry Arjun, "not in secret heroes fight,
Not behind a child or woman screen their valour and their might!

Krishna, loth is archer Arjun to pursue this hateful strife,
Trick against the sinless Bhishma, fraud upon his spotless life!

Knowest thou good and noble Krishna, as a child I climbed his knee,
As a boy I called him father, hung upon him lovingly?

Perish conquest! dearly purchased by a mean deceitful strife!
Perish crown and jewelled sceptre! won with Bhishma's saintly life!"

Gravely answered noble Krishna: "Bhishma falls by close of day,
Victim to the cause of virtue, he himself hath showed the way!

Dear or hated be the foeman, Arjun, thou shalt fight and slay,
Wherefore else the blood of nations hast thou poured from day to day?"

Morning dawned, and mighty Arjun, Abhimanyu young and bold,
Drupad monarch of Panchala, and Virata stern and old,

Brave Yudhishthir and his brothers clad in arms and shining mail,
Rushed to war where Bhishma's standard gleamed and glittered in
the gale!

Proud Duryodhan marked their onset, and its fatal purpose knew,
And his bravest men and chieftains 'gainst the fiery Pandavs threw,

With Kamboja's stalwart monarch and with Drona's mighty son,
With the valiant bowman Kripa stemmed the battle still unwon!

And his younger, fierce Duhsasan, thirsting for the deathful war,
'Gainst the helmet-wearing Arjun drew his mighty battle-car,

As a high and rugged mountain meets the angry ocean's sway,
Proud Duhsasan warred with Arjun in his wild and onward way,

And as myriad white-winged sea-birds swoop upon the darksome wave,
Clouds of darts and glistening lances drank the red blood of the brave!

Other warlike Kuru chieftains came, the bravest and the best,
Drona's self and Bhagadatta, monarch of the farthest East,

Car-borne Salya, mighty warrior, king of Madra's distant land,
Princes from Avanti's regions, chiefs from Malav's rocky strand,

Jayadratha, matchless fighter, king of Sindhu's sounding shore,
Chetrasena and Vikarna, countless chiefs and warriors more!

And they faced the fiery Pandavs, peerless in their warlike might,
Long and dreadful raged the combat, darkly closed the dubious fight,

Dust arose like clouds of summer, glistening darts like lightning played,
Darksome grew the sky with arrows, thicker grew the gloomy shade,

Cars went down and mailéd horsemen, soldiers fell in dread array,
Elephants with white tusks broken and with mangled bodies lay!

Arjun and the stalwart Bhima, piercing through their countless foes,
Side by side impelled their chariots, where the palm-tree standard rose!

Where the peerless ancient Bhishma on that dark and fatal day,
Warring with the banded nations, still resistless held his way!

On he came, his palm-tree standard still the front of battle knew,
And like sun from dark clouds parting Bhishma burst on Arjun's view!

And his eyes brave Arjun shaded at the awe-inspiring sight,
Half he wished to turn for shelter from that chief of godlike might!

But bold Krishna drove his chariot, whispered unto him his plan,
Arjun placed the young Sikhandin in the deathful battle's van!

Bhishma viewed the Pandav forces with a calm unmoving face,
Saw not Arjun's fair *gandiva*, saw not Bhima's mighty mace,

Smiled to see the young Sikhandin rushing to the battle's fore,
Like the foam upon the billow when the mighty storm-winds roar!

Bhishma thought of word he plighted, and of oath that he had sworn,
Dropped his arms before the warrior who was but a female born!

And the standard which no warrior ever saw in base retreat,
Idly stood upon the chariot, threw its shade on Bhishma's seat!

Then the flagstaff fell dissevered on the crushed and broken car,
As from azure sky of midnight falls the meteor's flaming star!

Not by young Sikhandin's arrows Bhishma's palm-tree standard fell,
Not Sikhandin's feeble lances did the peerless Bhishma quell,

True to oath the bleeding chieftain turned his darkening face away,
Turned and fell; the sun declining marked the closing of the day.

Ended thus the fatal battle, truce came with the close of day,
Kurus and the silent Pandavs went where Bhishma dying lay,

Arjun wept as for a father weeps the sad and sorrowing son,
Good Yudhishthir cursed the morning Kuru-kshetra's war begun,

Stood Duryodhan and his brothers mantled in the gloom of grief,
Foes like loving brothers sorrowed round the great, the dying chief!

Arjun's keen and pointed arrows made the hero's dying bed,
And in soft and gentle accents to Duryodhan thus he said:

"List unto my words, Duryodhan, uttered with my latest breath,
List to Bhishma's dying counsel and revere the voice of death!

End this dread and deathful battle if thy stony heart can grieve,
Save the chieftains doomed to slaughter, let the fated nations live!

Grant his kingdom to Yudhishthir, righteous man beloved of Heaven,
Keep thy own Hastina's regions, be the hapless past forgiven!"

Vain, alas! the voice of Bhishma like a heavenly warning spoke,
Hatred dearer than his life-blood in the proud Duryodhan woke!

Darker grew the gloomy midnight, and the princes went their way,
On his bed of pointed arrows Bhishma lone and dying lay,

Karna, though he loved not Bhishma whilst the chieftain lived in fame,
Gently to the dying Bhishma in the midnight darkness came!

Bhishma heard the tread of Karna, and he oped his glazing eye,
Spake in love and spake in sadness, and his bosom heaved a sigh:

"Pride and envy, noble Karna, filled our warlike hearts with strife,
Discord ends with breath departing, envy sinks with fleeting life!

More I have to tell thee, Karna, but my parting breath may fail,
Feeble are my dying accents, and my parchéd lips are pale!

Arjun beats not noble Karna in the deeds of valour done,
Nor excels in birth and lineage, Karna, thou art Pritha's son!

Pritha bore thee, still unwedded, and the Sun inspired thy birth,
God-born man! No mightier archer treads this broad and spacious
earth!

Pritha cast thee in her sorrow, hid thee with a maiden's shame,
And a driver, not thy father, nursed thee, chief of warlike fame!

Arjun is thy brother, Karna, end this sad fraternal war,
Seek not life-blood of thy brother, nor against him drive thy car!"

Vain, alas! the voice of Bhishma like a heavenly warning spoke,
Hatred dearer than his life-blood in the vengeful Karna woke!

BOOK IX

DRONA-BADHA

(Fall of Drona)

ON the fall of Bhishma the Brahman chief Drona, preceptor of the Kuru and Pandav princes, was appointed the leader of the Kuru forces. For five days Drona held his own against the Pandavs, and some of the incidents of these days, like the fall of Abhimanyu and the vengeance of Arjun, are among the most stirring passages in the Epic. The description of the different standards of the Pandav and the Kuru warriors is also interesting. At last Drona slew his ancient foe the king of the Panchalas, and was then slain by his son the prince of the Panchalas.

The Book is an abridgment of Book vii. of the original text.

I

Single Combat between Bhima and Salya

Morning ushered in the battle; Pandav warriors heard with dread
Drona, priest and proud preceptor, now the Kuru forces led!

And the foe-compelling Drona pledged his troth and solemn word,
He would take Yudhishthir captive to Hastina's haughty lord!

But the ever faithful Arjun to his virtuous elder bowed,
And in clear and manful accents spake his warlike thoughts aloud:

"Sacred is our great preceptor, sacred is *acharya's* life,
Arjun may not slay his teacher even in this mortal strife!

Saving this, command, O monarch, Arjun's bow and warlike sword,
For thy safety, honoured elder, Arjun stakes his plighted word!

Matchless in the art of battle is our teacher fierce and dread,
But he comes not to Yudhishthir save o'er blood of Arjun shed!"

Morning witnessed doughty Drona foremost in the battle's tide,
But Yudhishthir's warlike chieftains compassed him on every side,

Foremost of the youthful chieftains came resistless Arjun's son,—
Father's blood and milk of mother fired his deeds of valour done,

As the lion of the jungle drags the ox into his lair,
Abhimanyu from his chariot dragged Paurava by his hair!

Jayadratha king of Sindhu marked the faint and bleeding chief,
Leaping from his car of battle, wrathful came to his relief,

Abhimanyu left his captive, turned upon the mightier foe,
And with sword and hardened buckler gave and parried many a blow,

Rank to rank from both the forces cry of admiration rose,
Streaming men poured forth in wonder, watched the combat fierce
and close!

Piercing Abhimanyu's buckler Jayadratha sent his stroke,
But the turned and twisted sword-blade snapping in the midway broke,

Weaponless the king of Sindhu ran into his sheltering car,
Salya came unto his rescue from a battle-field afar,

Dauntless, on the new assailant, Arjun's son his weapon drew,
Interposing 'twixt the fighters Bhima's self on Salya flew!

Stoutest wrestlers in the armies, peerless fighters with the mace,
Bhima and the stalwart Salya stood opposéd face to face!

Hempen fastening bound their maces and the wire of twisted gold,
Whirling bright, like circling flashes, shook their staffs the warriors
bold!

Oft they struck, and sparks of red fire issued from the seasoned wood,
And like hornéd bulls infuriate Madra's king and Bhima stood!

Closer still they came like tigers closing with their reddened paws,
Or like tuskers in the jungle, eagles with their rending claws!

Loud as INDRA's peals of thunder still their blows were echoed round,
Rank to rank the startled soldiers heard the oft-repeated sound!

But as strikes in vain the lightning on the solid mountain-rock,
Bhima nor the fearless Salya fell or moved beneath the shock!

Closer drew the watchful heroes, and their clubs were wielded well,
Till by many blows belaboured both the fainting fighters fell!

Like a drunkard dazed and reeling Bhima rose his staff to wield,
Senseless Salya, heavy-breathing, henchman carried from the field!

Writhing like a wounded serpent, lifted from the field of war,
He was carried by his soldiers to the shelter of his car!

Drona still with matchless prowess would redeem his plighted word,
Sought to take Yudhishthir captive to Duryodhan, Kuru's lord,

Vainly then the twin-born brothers came to cross the conqueror's path,
Matsya's lord, Panchala's monarch, vainly faced him in his wrath,

Rank to rank the cry resounded circling o'er the battle-field,
"Drona takes Yudhishthir captive with his weapons, sword and shield!"

Arjun heard the dreadful message and in haste and fury came,
Strove to save his king and elder and redeem his loyal fame,

Speeding with his milk-white coursers dashed into the thick of war,
Blew his shrill and dreaded *sankha*, drove his sounding battle-car,

Fiercer, darker grew the battle, when above the reddened plain,
Evening drew her peaceful mantle o'er the living and the slain!

II

Standards of the Pandavs

Morning came; still round Yudhishthir Drona led the gathering war,
Arjun fought the Sam-saptakas in a battle-field afar,

But the prince of fair Panchala marked his father's ancient foe,
And against the doughty Drona, Dhrishta-dyumna bent his bow!

But as darksome cloudy masses angry gusts of storm divide,
Through the scattered, fainting foemen Drona drove his car in pride,

Steeds went down and riven chariots, young Panchala turned and fled,
Onward drove resistless Drona through the dying and the dead!

One more prince of fair Panchala 'gainst the mighty Drona came,—
Ancient feud ran in the red blood of Panchala's chiefs of fame,—

Fated youth! with reckless valour still he fought his father's foe,
Fought and fell; relentless Drona laid the brave Satyajit low!

Surging still like ocean's billows other Pandav warriors came,
To protect their virtuous monarch and redeem their ancient fame,

Came in various battle-chariots drawn by steeds of every hue,
Various were the chieftains' standards which the warring nations knew!

Bhima drove his stalwart horses tinted like the dappled deer,
Grey and pigeon-coloured coursers bore Panchala's prince and peer,

Horses bred in famed Kamboja, fiery, parrot-green in hue,
Brave Nakula's sumptuous chariot in the deathful battle drew,

Piebald horses trained to battle did young Sahadeva rein,
Ivory-white Yudhishthir's coursers with their flowing ebon mane,

And by him with gold umbrella valiant monarch Drupad came,
Horses of a bright-bay colour carried Matsya's king of fame.

Varied as their various coursers gallantly their standards rose,
With their wondrous strange devices, terror of their arméd foes!

Water-jar on tawny deerskin, such was Drona's sign of war,—
Drona as a tender infant rested in a water-jar,

Golden moon with stars surrounding was Yudhishthir's sign of yore,
Silver lion was the standard tiger-waisted Bhima bore,

Brave Nakula's sign was red deer with its back of burnished gold,
Silver swan with bells resounding Sahadeva's onset told,

Golden peacock rich-emblazoned was young Abhimanyu's joy,
Vulture shone on Ghatotkacha, Bhima's proud and gallant boy.

Now Duryodhan marked the foemen heaving like the rising tide,
And he faced the wrathful Bhima towering in his tameless pride,

Short the war, for proud Duryodhan wounded from the battle fled,
And his warriors from fair Anga rested with the countless dead!

Wild with anger Bhagadatta, monarch of the farthest East,
With his still unconquered forces on the valiant Bhima pressed,

Came from far the wrathful Arjun, and the battle's front he sought,
Where by eastern foes surrounded still the stalwart Bhima fought!

Fated monarch from the far-east Brahma-putra's sounding shore,
Land of rising sun will hail him and his noble peers no more,

For his tusker pierced by arrows trumpeted his dying wail,
Like a red and flaming meteor gallant Bhagadatta fell!

Then with rising wrath and anguish Karna's noble bosom bled,—
Karna, who had stayed from battle while his rival Bhishma led,

Ancient hate and jealous anger clouded Karna's warlike heart,
And while Bhishma led, all idly slumbered Karna's bow and dart!

Now he marked with warrior's anguish all his comrades fled afar,
And his foeman Arjun sweeping o'er the red field of the war,

Anger like a tongue of red fire shot from Karna's flaming eye,
And he sprang to meet his foemau or to conquer or to die!

Fierce and dubious was the battle, answering clouds gave back the din,
Karna met his dearest foeman, and, alas! his nearest kin!

Bhima and Panchala's warriors unto Arjun's rescue came,
Proud Duryodhan came to Karna, and fair Sindhu's king of fame!

Fiercely raged the gory combat, when the night its shadows threw,
Wounded men and blood-stained chieftains to their nightly tents withdrew!

III

Abhimanyu's Death

Fatal was the blood-red morning purpling o'er the angry east,
Fatal day for Abhimanyu, bravest warrior and the best!

Countless were the gallant chieftains like the sands beside the sea,
None with braver bosom battled, none with hands more stout and free!

Brief, alas! thy radiant summers, fair Subhadra's gallant boy,
Loved of Matsya's soft-eyed princess and her young heart's pride and joy!

Brief, alas! thy sunlit winters, light of war too early quenched,
Peerless son of peerless Arjun, in the blood of foemen drenched!

Drona on that fatal morning ranged his dreadful battle-line
In a circle darkly spreading where the chiefs with chiefs combine,

And the Pandavs looked despairing on the battle's dread array,
Vainly strove to force a passage, vainly sought their onward way!

Abhimanyu, young and fiery, dashed alone into the war,
Reckless through the shattered forces all resistless drove his car,

Elephants and crashing standards, neighing steeds and warriors slain
Fell before the furious hero as he made a ghastly lane!

Proud Duryodhan rushed to battle, strove to stop the turning tide,
And his stoutest, truest warriors fought by proud Duryodhan's side,

Onward still went Abhimanyu, Kurus strove and fought in vain,
Backward reeled and fell Duryodhan, and his bravest chiefs were slain!

Next came Salya, car-borne monarch, 'gainst the young resistless foe,
Urged his fiery battle-coursers, stretched his dread unerring bow,

Onward still went Ahhimanyu, Salya strove and fought in vain,
And his warriors took him bleeding from the reddened battle-plain!

Next Duhsasan darkly lowering thundered with his bended bow,
Abhimanyu smiled to see him, kinsman and the dearest foe,

"Art thou he," said Abhimanyu, "known for cruel word and deed,
Impious in thy heart and purpose, base and ruthless in thy greed?

Didst thou with the false Sakuni win a realm by low device,
Win his kingdom from Yudhishthir by ignoble trick of dice?

Didst thou in the council chamber with your insults foul and keen
By her flowing raven tresses drag Yudhishthir's stainless queen?

Didst thou speak to warlike Bhima as thy serf and bounden slave,
Wrong my father, righteous Arjun, peerless prince and warrior brave?

Welcome! I have sought thee often, wished to cross thy tainted path,
Welcome! Dearest of all victims to my nursed and cherished wrath!

Reap the meed of sin and insult, draw on earth thy latest breath,
For I owe to Queen Draupadi, impious prince, thy speedy death!"

Like a snake upon an ant-hill, on Duhsasan's wicked heart,
Fell with hissing wrath and fury Abhimanyu's fiery dart!

From the loss of blood Duhsasan fainted on his battle-car,
Kuru chieftains bore him senseless from the blood-stained scene of war!

Next in gleaming arms accoutred came Duryodhan's gallant son,
Proud and warlike as his father, famed for deeds of valour done,

Young in years and rich in valour, for, alas! he fought too well,
And before his weeping father proud and gallant Lakshman fell!

Onward still went Abhimanyu midst the dying and the dead,
Shook from rank to rank the Kurus and their shattered army fled!

Then the impious Jayadratha, king of Sindhu's sounding shore,
Came forth in unrighteous concert with six car-borne warriors more,

Darkly closed the fatal circle with the gulfing surge's moan,
Dauntless, with the seven brave chieftains Abhimanyu fought alone!

Fell, alas! his peacock standard, and his car was broke in twain,
Bow and sabre rent and shattered, and his faithful driver slain,

Heedless yet of death and danger, misty with the loss of blood,
Abhimanyu wiped his forehead, gazed where dark his foemen stood!

Then with wild despairing valour, flickering flame of closing life,
Mace in hand the heedless warrior rushed to end the mortal strife,

Rushed upon his startled foemen, Abhimanyu fought and fell!
And his deeds to distant ages bards and wand'ring minstrels tell!

Like a tusker of the forest by surrounding hunters slain,
Like a wood-consuming wildfire quenched upon the distant plain,

Like a mountain-shaking tempest, spent in force and hushed and still,
Like the red resplendent day-god setting on the western hill,

Like the moon serene and beauteous quenched in eclipse, dark and pale,
Lifeless slumbered Abhimanyu when the softened starlight fell!

Done the day of death and slaughter, darkening shadows close around,
Wearied warriors seek for shelter on the vast and tented ground,

Soldiers' camp-fires brightly blazing, tent-lights shining from afar,
Cast their fitful gleam and radiance on the carnage of the war!

अभिमन्युः।

Abhimanyu on foot.

Arjun from a field at distance, where upon that day he fought,
With the ever faithful Krishna now his nightly shelter sought,

"Wherefore, Krishna," uttered Arjun, "evil omens strike my eye,
Thoughts of sadness fill my bosom, wake the long-forgotten sigh?

Wherefore voice of evening bugle speaks not on the battle-field,
Merry conch nor sounding trumpet music to the warriors yield?

Harp is hushed within the dark tents and the voice of warlike song,
Bards beside the evening camp-fire tales of war do not prolong!

Good Yudhishthir's tent is voiceless, and my brothers look so pale,
Abhimanyu comes not joyous Krishna and his sire to hail!

Abhimanyu's love and greeting bless like blessings from above,
Fair Subhadra's joy and treasure, Arjun's pride and hope and love!"

Softly and with many tear-drops did the sad Yudhishthir tell,
How in dreadful field of battle gallant Abhimanyu fell!

How the impious Jayadratha fell on Arjun's youthful son,—
He with six proud Kuru chieftains,—Abhimanyu all alone!

How the young prince, reft of weapon and deprived of steed and car,
Fell as falls a Kshatra warrior fighting on the field of war!

Arjun heard; the father's bosom throbbed with pain of cureless wound,
"Brave and gallant boy!" said Arjun;—and he sank upon the ground!

Moments passed of voiceless sorrow and of speechless bitter tear,
Sobs within his mailéd bosom smote the weeping listener's ear!

Moments passed; with rising anger quivered Arjun's iron frame,
Abhimanyu's cruel murder smote the father's heart to flame!

"Didst thou say that Sindhu's monarch on my Abhimanyu bore,—
He alone,—and Jayadratha leagued with six maurauders more?

Didst thou say the impious Kurus stooped unto this deed of shame,
Outrage on the laws of honour, stain upon a warrior's fame?

Father's curse, a warrior's hatred sting them to their dying breath,
For they feared my boy in battle, hunted him to cruel death!

Hear my vow, benign Yudhishthir, hear me, Krishna, righteous lord,
Arjun's hand shall slay the slayer, Arjun plights his solemn word!

May I never reach the bright sky where the righteous fathers dwell,
May I with the darkest sinners live within the deepest hell,—

Parricides who slay their fathers, shed their loving mothers' blood,
Stain the sacred bed of *gurus*, steal their gold and holy food,

Cherish envy, cheat their kinsmen, speak the low and dastard lie,—
If, ere comes to-morrow's sunset, Jayadratha doth not die!

Jayadratha dies to-morrow, victim to my vengeful ire,
Arjun else shall yield his weapons, perish on the flaming pyre!"

Softer tear-drops wept the mother, joyless was Subhadra's life,—
Krishna's fair and honoured sister, Arjun's dear and lovéd wife:

"Dost thou lie on field of battle, smeared with dust and foeman's gore,
Child of light and love and sweetness whom thy hapless mother bore?

Soft thine eye as budding lotus, sweet and gentle was thy face,
Are those soft eyes closed in slumber, faded is that peerless grace?

And thy limbs so young and tender, on the bare earth do they lie,
Where the hungry jackal prowleth and the vulture flutters nigh?

Gold and jewels graced thy bosom, gems bedecked thy lofty crest,
Doth the crimson mark of sabre decorate that manly breast?

Rend Subhadra's stony bosom with a mother's cureless grief,
Let her follow Abhimanyu and in death obtain relief!

Earth to me is void and cheerless, joyless is my hearth and home,
Dreary without Abhimanyu is this weary world to roam!

And oh! cheerless is that young heart, Abhimanyu's princess-wife,
What can sad Subhadra offer to her joyless, sunless life?

Close our life in equal darkness, for our day on earth is done,
For our love and light and treasure, Abhimanyu dead and gone!"

Long bewailed the anguished mother, fair Draupadi tore her hair,
Matsya's princess, early widowed, shed her young heart's blood in tear!

IV

Standards of the Kurus: Arjun's Revenge

Morning from the face of battle night's depending curtain drew,
Long and shrill his sounding *sankha* then the wrathful Arjun blew!

Kurus knew the vow of Arjun, heard the *sankha's* deathful blare,
As it rose above the red field, thrilled the startled morning air!

"Speed, my Krishna," out spake Arjun, as aloft he held his bow,
"For to-day my task is dreadful, cruel is my mighty vow!"

Fiery coursers urged by Krishna flew with ligntning's rapid course,
Dashing through the hostile warriors and the serried Kuru force!

Brave Durmarsan faced the hero, but he strove and fought in vain,
Onward thundered Arjun's chariot o'er the dying and the slain!

Fierce Duhsasan with his tuskers rushed into the line of war,
But the tuskers broke in panic, onward still went Arjun's car!

Drona then, the proud preceptor, Arjun's furious progress stayed,
Tear-drops filled the eye of Arjun as these gentle words he said:

"Pardon, father! if thy pupil shuns to-day thy offered war,
'Gainst his Abhimanyu's slayer Arjun speeds his battle-car!

Not against my great *acharya* is my wrathful bow-string drawn,
Not against a lovéd father fights a loving duteous son!

Heavy on this bleeding bosom sits the darkening load of woe,
And an injured father's vengeance seeks the slaughtered hero's foe!

Pardon then if sorrowing Arjun seeks a far and distant way,
Mighty is the vow of Arjun, cruel is his task to-day!"

Passing by the doughty Drona onward sped the fiery car,
Through the broken line of warriors, through the shattered ranks of war,

Angas and the brave Kalingas vainly crossed his wrathful way,
Proud Avantis from the regions where fair Chambal's waters stray!

Famed Avanti's fated princes vainly led their highland force,
Fell beneath the wrath of Arjun, stayed nor stopped his onward course,

Onward still with speed of lightning thundered Arjun's battle-car,
To the spot where Jayadratha stood behind the ranks of war!

Now the sun from highest zenith red and fiery radiance lent,
Long and weary was the passage, Arjun's foaming steeds were spent,

"Arjun!" said the faithful Krishna, "arduous is thy cruel quest,
But thy foaming coursers falter, and they need a moment's rest,"

"Be it so," brave Arjun answered, "from our chariot we alight,
Rest awhile the weary horses, Krishna, I will watch the fight!"

Speaking thus the arméd Arjun lightly leaped upon the lea,
Stood on guard with bow and arrow by the green and shady tree,

Krishna groomed the jaded horses, faint and feeble, red with gore,
With a healing hand he tended wounds the bleeding coursers bore,

Watered them beside a river by the zephyrs soft caressed,
Gave unto them welcome fodder, gave unto them needful rest,

Thus refreshed, the noble coursers Krishna harnessed to the car,
And the gleaming helméd Arjun rushed once more into the war!

Came on him the Kuru warriors, darksome wave succeeding wave,
Standards decked with strange devices, streaming banners rich and brave,

Foremost was the glorious standard of preceptor Drona's son,
Lion's tail in golden brilliance on his battle-chariot shone,

Elephant's rope was Karna's ensign made of rich and burnished gold,
And a bull bedecked the standard of the bowman Kripa bold,

Peacock made of precious metal, decked with jewels rich and rare,
Vrishasena's noble standard shone aloft serene and fair,

Ploughshare of a golden lustre, shining like the radiant flame,
Spoke the car of mighty Salya, Madra's king of warlike fame,

Far, and guarded well by chieftains, shone the dazzling silver-boar,
Ensign proud of Jayadratha, brought from Sindhu's sounding shore,

On the car of Somadatta shone a stake of sacrifice,
Silver boar and golden parrots, these were Salwa's proud device,

Last and brightest of the standards, on the prince Duryodhan's car,
Lordly elephant in jewels proudly shone above the war!

Nine heroic Kuru chieftains, bravest warriors and the best,
Leagued they came to grapple Arjun and on faithful Krishna pressed!

Arjun swept like sweeping whirlwind, all resistless in his force,
Sought no foe and waged no combat, held his ever onward course!

For he sighted Jayadratha midst the circling chiefs of war,
'Gainst that warrior, grim and silent, Arjun drove his furious car!

Now the day-god rolled his chariot on the western clouds aflame,
Karna's self and five great chieftains round brave Jayadratha came,

Vainly strove the valiant Arjun struggling 'gainst the Kuru line,
Charged upon the peerless Karna as he marked the day's decline,

Krishna then a prayer whispered; came a friendly sable cloud,
Veiled the red sun's dazzling brilliance in a dark and inky shroud!

Karna deemed the evening darkness now proclaimed the close of strife,
Failing in his plighted promise Arjun must surrender life,

And his comrade chiefs rejoicing slackened in their furious fight,
Jayadratha hailed with gladness thickening shades of welcome night!

In that sad and fatal error all the Kuru chiefs combine,
Arjun quick as bolt of lightning breaks their all unguarded line,

Like an onward sweeping wildfire shooting forth its lolling tongue,
On the startled Jayadratha Arjun in his fury flung!

Short the strife; as angry falcon swoops upon its helpless prey,
Arjun sped his vengeful arrow, and his foeman lifeless lay!

Friendly winds removed the dark cloud from the reddening western hill,
And the sun in crimson lustre cast its fiery radiance still!

Ere the evening's mantling darkness fell o'er distant hill and plain,
Proud Duryodhan's many brothers were by vengeful Bhima slain,

And Duryodhan, stung by sorrow, waged the still unceasing fight,
In the thick and gathering darkness torches lit the gloom of night!

Karna, furious in his anger for his Jayadratha slain,
And for brothers of Duryodhan sleeping lifeless on the plain,

'Gainst the gallant son of Bhima drove his dread resounding car,
And in gloom and midnight darkness waked the echoes of the war!

Bhima's son brave Ghatotkacha twice proud Karna's horses slew,
Twice the humbled steedless Karna from the dubious battle flew,

Came again the fiery Karna, vengeance flamed within his heart,
Like the midnight's lurid lightning sped his fell and fatal dart!

Woeful was the hour of darkness, luckless was the starry sway,
Bhima's son in youth and valour lifeless on the red field lay!

Then was closed the midnight battle, silent shone the starry light,
Bhima knew nor rest nor slumber through the long and woeful night!

V

Fall of Drona

Ere the crimson morning glittered proud Duryodhan sad at heart,
To the leader of the Kurus did his sorrows thus impart:

"Sadly speeds the contest, Drona, on the battle's gory plain,
Kuru chiefs are thinned and fallen and my brothers mostly slain!

Can it be, O best of Brahmans! peerless in the art of war,
Can it be that we shall falter while thou speed'st the battle-car?

Pandu's sons are but thy pupils, Arjun meets thee not in fight,
None can face the great *acharya* in his wrath and warlike might!

Wherefore then in every battle are the Kuru chieftains slain,
Wherefore lie my warlike brothers lifeless on the ghastly plain?

Is it that the fates of battle 'gainst the Kuru house combine,
Is it that thy heart's affection unto Pandu's sons incline?

If thy secret love and mercy still the sons of Pandu claim,
Yield thy place to gallant Karna, Anga's prince of warlike fame!"

Answered Drona brief and wrathful: "Fair Gandhari's royal son,
Reapest thou the gory harvest of thy sinful actions done!

Cast no blame in youth's presumption on a warrior's fleecy hair,
Faithful unto death is Drona, to his plighted promise fair!

Ask thyself, O prince Duryodhan! bound by battle's sacred laws,
Wherefore fightest not with Arjun for thy house and for thy cause?

Ask the dark and deep Sakuni, where is now his low device,
Wherefore wields he not his weapon as he wields the loaded dice?

Ask the chief who proudly boasted, archer Arjun he would slay,
Helméd Arjun sways the battle, whither now doth Karna stay?

Know the truth; the gallant Arjun hath no peer on earth below,
And no warrior breathes, Duryodhan, who can face thy helméd foe!

Drona knows his sacred duty; and 'tis willed by Heaven on high,
Arjun or preceptor Drona shall in this day's battle die!"

Now the sun in crimson splendour rolled his car of glistening gold,
Sent his shafts of purple radiance on the plain and mountain bold,

And from elephant and charger, from their bravely bannered car,
Lighted mailéd kings and chieftains and the serried hosts of war,

Faced the sun with hands conjoinéd and the sacred *mantra* told,—
Hymns by ancient *rishis* chanted, sanctified by bards of old!

Worship done, each silent warrior mounts the car or battle-steed,
Onward to the deathful contest doth his gallant forces lead,

Ill it fared with Pandav forces, doughty Drona took the field,
Peer was none midst living warriors of the Brahman trained and
skilled!

Arjun, faithful to his promise, his preceptor would not fight,
King nor chief nor other archer dared to face his peerless might,

But old feud like potent poison fires the warrior's heart with strife,
Sire to son still unforgotten leaps the hate from death to life!

Wrathful princes of Panchala, by their deathless hatred stung,
Saw their ancient foe in Drona and on him for vengeance sprung!

Darkly thought the ancient warrior of the old relentless feud,
Fiercely like a jungle-tiger fell upon the hostile brood!

Royal Drupad's valiant grandsons in their youth untimely slain,
Victims of a deathless discord, pressed the gory battle-plain!

Drupad pale with grief and anger marked his gallant grandsons dead,
And his army broken, routed, and his bravest chieftains fled,

Filled with unforgotten hatred and with father's grief and pride,
Rushed the king, and bold Virata charged by doughty Drupad's
side!

Rose a cry of nameless terror o'er the red and ghastly plain,
Noble Drupad, brave Virata, lay among the countless slain!

Burning tears the proud Draupadi wept for noble father killed,
Maid and matron with their wailing fair Panchala's empire filled!

Matsya's joyless, widowed princess, for her fate was early crost,
Wept with added tears and anguish for her father loved and lost!

Waged the war with fearful slaughter, Drona onward urged his way,
Fate alone and battle's chances changed the fortunes of the day,

Aswa-thaman, son of Drona, was a chief of peerless fame,
And an elephant of battle bore that chieftain's warlike name,

And that proud and lordly tusker, Bhima in his prowess slew,
Rank to rank, from friend to foeman, then a garbled message flew:

"Aswa-thaman son of Drona is by mighty Bhima slain!"
Drona heard that fatal message, bent his anguished head in pain!

"Speak, Yudhishthir, soul of virtue!" thus the proud preceptor cried,
"Thou in truth hast never faltered, and thy lips have never lied!

Speak of valiant Aswa-thaman, Drona's hope and pride and joy,
Hath he fallen in this battle, is he slain, my gallant boy?

Feeble are the hands of Drona and his prowess quenched and gone,
Fleecy are his ancient tresses and his earthly task is done!"

Said Yudhishthir: "Lordly tusker, Aswa-thaman named, is dead,"
Drona heard but half the accents, feebly drooped his sinking head!

Then the prince of fair Panchala swiftly drove across the plain,
Marked his father's cruel slayer, marked his noble father slain!

Dhrista-dyumna bent his weapon and his shaft was pointed well,
And the priest and proud preceptor, peerless Drona lifeless fell!

And the fatal day was ended, Kurus fled in abject fear,
Arjun for his ancient teacher dropped a silent filial tear!

BOOK X

KARNA-BADHA

(Fall of Karna)

KARNA was chosen as the leader of the Kuru forces after the death of Drona, and held his own for two days. The great contest between Karna and Arjun, long expected and long deferred, came on at last. It is the crowning incident of the Indian Epic, as the contest between Hector and Achilles is the crowning incident of the Iliad. With a truer artistic skill than that of Homer, the Indian poet represents Karna as equal to Arjun in strength and skill, and his defeat is only due to an accident.

After the death of Karna, Salya led the Kuru troops on the eighteenth and last day of the war, and fell. A midnight slaughter in the Pandav camp, perpetrated by the vengeful son of Drona, concludes the war. Duryodhan, left wounded by Bhima, heard of the slaughter and died happy.

Books viii., ix., and x. of the original have been abridged in this Book.

I

Karna and Arjun meet

Sights of red and ghastly carnage day disclosed upon the plain,
Mighty chiefs and countless warriors round the warlike Drona slain!

Sad Duryodhan gazed in sorrow and the tear was in his eye,
Till his glances fell on Karna and his warlike heart beat high!

"Karna!" so exclaimed Duryodhan, "hero of resistless might,
Thou alone canst serve the Kuru in this dread and dubious fight,

Step forth, Kuru's chief and leader! mount thy sounding battle-car,
Lead the still unconquered Kurus to the trophies of the war!

Matchless was the ancient Bhishma in this famed and warlike land,
But a weakness for Yudhishthir palsied Bhishma's slaying hand,

Matchless too was doughty Drona in the warrior's skill and art,
Kindness for his pupil Arjun lurked within the teacher's heart!

Greater than the ancient grandsire, greater than the Brahman old,
Fiercer in thy deathless hatred, stronger in thy prowess bold,

Peerless Karna! lead us onward to a brighter, happier fate,
For thy arm is nerved to action by an unforgotten hate!

Lead us as the martial SKANDA led the conquering gods of old,
Smite the foe as angry INDRA smote the Danavs fierce and bold,

As before the light of morning flies the baleful gloom of night,
Pandavs and the proud Panchalas fly before thy conquering might!"

Priests with hymns and chanted *mantra* and with every sacred rite
Hailed him Leader of the Kurus, chieftain of unconquered might,

Earthen jars they placed around him with the sacred water full,
Elephant's tusk they laid beside him and the horn of mighty bull,

Gem and jewel, corn and produce, by the armèd hero laid,
Silken cloth of finest lustre o'er his crested head they spread,

Brahmans poured the holy water, bards his lofty praises sung,
Kshatras, Vaisyas, purer Sudras hailed him Leader bold and strong!

"Vanquish warlike sons of Pritha!" thus the holy Brahmans blessed,
Gold and garments, food and cattle, joyous Karna on them pressed!

Thus the holy rite concluded, Karna ranged his men in war,
To the dreaded front of battle drove his swift and conquering
car!

Morn to noon and noon to evening raged the battle on the plain,
Countless warriors fought and perished, car-borne chiefs were pierced and slain!

Helméd Arjun, crested Karna, met at last by will of fate,
Life-long was their mutual anger, deathless was their mutual hate!

And the firm earth shook and trembled 'neath the furious rush of war,
And the echoing welkin answered shouts that nations heard from far!

And the darkening cloud of arrows filled the firmament on high,
Darker, deeper, dread and deadlier, grew the angry face of sky!

Till the evening's sable garment mantled o'er the battle-field,
And the angry rivals parted, neither chief could win or yield!

II

Fall of Karna

At the break of morning Karna unto prince Duryodhan went,
Thus in slow and measured accents to his inner thoughts gave vent:

"Morning dawns, O Kuru's monarch! mighty Arjun shall be slain,
Or fulfilling warrior's duty Karna dyes the gory plain!

Long through life within our bosoms ever burnt the mutual hate,
Oft we met and often parted, rescued by the will of fate!

But yon sun with crimson lustre sees us meet to part no more,
Gallant Arjun's course this evening or proud Karna's shall be o'er!

Room is none for Arjun's glory and for archer Karna's fame,
One must sink and one must sparkle with a brighter, richer flame!

List yet more; in wealth of weapons and in wondrous strength of bow,
Arjun scarcely me surpasseth, scarcely I excel my foe!

In the light skill of the archer and in sight and truth of aim,
Arjun beats not, scarcely rivals, Karna's proud and peerless fame!

If his wondrous bow *gandiva* is the gift of gods in heaven,
Karna's bow the famed *vijaya* is by Par'su-Rama given!

Ay! the son of Jamadagni, kings of earth who proudly slayed,
On the youthful arms of Karna his destructive weapon laid!

Yet I own, O king of Kuru! Arjun doth his foe excel,—
Matchless are his fiery coursers, peerless Krishna leads them well!

Krishna holds the reins for Arjun, Krishna speeds his battle-car,
Drives the lightning-wingéd coursers o'er the startled field of war!

Sweeps in pride his sounding chariot till it almost seems to fly,
Arjun lords it o'er the battle like the comet in the sky!

Grant me, monarch, mighty Salya drive my swift and warlike steed,
And against the car-borne Arjun, Karna's fiery chariot lead!

Salya too is skilled, like Krishna, with the steed and battle-car,
Equal thus I meet my foeman in this last and fatal war!"

Spake Duryodhan; warlike Salya mounted Karna's sounding car,
Karna sought for mighty Arjun in the serried ranks of war:

"Hundred milch-kine Karna offers, costly garment, yellow gold,
Unto him who in this battle points to me my foeman bold!

Cars and steeds and fertile acres, peaceful hamlets rich and fair,
Dark-eyed damsels, lotus-bosomed, crowned with glossy raven hair!

These are his who points to Karna, Arjun hiding from this war,
Arjun's snowy steeds and banner and his swift and thund'ring car!"

Karna spake, but long and loudly laughed the king of Madra's land,
As he reined the fiery coursers with his strong and skilful hand,

"Of rewards and gifts," he uttered, "little need is there, I ween,
Arjun is not wont to tarry from the battle's glorious scene!

Soon will Arjun's snowy coursers shake the battle's startled field,
Helméd Arjun like a comet gleam with bow and sword and shield!

As the forest-ranging tiger springs upon his fated prey,
As the hornéd bull, infuriate, doth the weakling cattle slay,

As the fierce and lordly lion smites the timid jungle-deer,
Arjun soon shall spring upon thee, for he knows nor dread nor fear,

Save thee, then, O mighty archer! while I drive my sounding car,
Pandu's son hath met no equal in the valiant art of war!"

Darkly frowned the angry Karna, Salya held the loosened rein,
Dashing through the hostile forces then the warrior drove amain,

Through the serried ranks of battle Karna drove in furious mood,
Facing him in royal splendour good Yudhishthir fearless stood!

Surging ranks of brave Nishadas closed between and fought in vain,
Proud Panchalas, stout and faithful, vainly strove among the slain,

Onward came the fiery Karna like the ocean's heaving swell,
With the sweeping wrath of tempest on the good Yudhishthir fell!

Wrathful then the son of Pandu marked his noblest chieftains dead,
And in words of scornful anger thus to archer Karna said:

"Hast thou, Karna, vowed the slaughter of my younger Arjun brave?
Wilt thou do Duryodhan's mandate, proud Duryodhan's willing slave?

Unfulfilled thy vow remaineth, for the righteous gods ordain,
By Yudhishthir's hand thou fallest, go and slumber with the slain!"

Fiercely drew his bow Yudhishthir, fiercely was the arrow driven,
Rocky cliff or solid mountain might the shaft have pierced and riven!

Lightning-like it came on Karna, struck him in the bleeding left,
And the warrior fell and fainted as of life and sense bereft!

Soon he rose; the cloud of anger darkened o'er his livid face,
And he drew his godlike weapon with a more than human grace!

Arrows keen and dark as midnight, gleaming in their lightning flight,
Struck Yudhishthir's royal armour with a fierce resistless might!

Clanking fell the shattered armour from his person fair and pale,
As from sun's meridian splendour clouds are drifted by the gale!

Armourless but bright and radiant brave Yudhishthir waged the fight,
Bright as sky with stars bespangled on a clear and cloudless night!

And he threw his pointed lances like the summer's bursting flood,
Once again Yudhishthir's weapons drank his fiery foeman's blood!

Pale with anguish, wrathful Karna fiercely turned the tide of war,
Cut Yudhishthir's royal standard, crushed his sumptuous battle-car!

And he urged his gallant coursers till his chariot bounding flew,
And with godlike prowess Karna then his famed *vijaya* drew!

Faint Yudhishthir sorely bleeding waged no more the fatal fight,
Carless, steedless, void of armour, sought his safety in his flight!

"Speed thou, timid man of penance!" proud insulting Karna said,
"Famed for virtue, not for valour! blood of thine I will not shed!

Speed and chant thy wonted *mantra*, do the rites that sages know,
Bid the helméd warrior Arjun come and meet his warlike foe!"

To his tent retired Yudhishthir in his wrath and in his shame,
Arjun from a distant battle to his angry elder came:

"Hast thou yet, O tardy Arjun! base, insulting Karna slain,
Karna dealing dire destruction on this battle's reddened plain?

Like his teacher Par'su-Rama dyes in purple blood his course,
Like a snake of deathful poison jealous guards the Kuru force!

Karna smote my chariot-driver and my standard rent in twain,
Shattered car and lifeless horses strew the red inglorious plain!

Scarce with life in speechless anguish from the battle-field I fled,
Scorn of foes and shame of kinsmen! Warrior's fame and honour dead!

Ten long years and three Yudhishthir joy nor peace nor rest hath seen,
And while Karna lives and glories, all our insults still are green!

Hast thou, Arjun, slain that chieftain as in swelling pride he stood,
Hast thou wiped our wrongs and insults in that chariot-driver's blood?"

"At a distance," Krishna answered, "fiery Arjun fought his way,
Now he meets the archer Karna, and he vows his death to-day."

Anger lit Yudhishthir's forehead, and a tremor shook his frame,
As he spake to silent Arjun words of insult and of shame:

"Wherefore like a painted warrior doth the helméd Arjun stand,
Wherefore useless lies *gandiva* in his weak and nerveless hand,

Wherefore hangs yon mighty sabre from his belt of silk and gold,
Wherefore drives the peerless Krishna Arjun's coursers fleet and bold,

If afar from war's arena timid Arjun seeks to hide,
If he shuns the mighty Karna battling in unconquered pride?

Arjun! yield thy famed *gandiva* unto worthier hands than thine,
On some braver, truer warrior let thy mighty standard shine,

Yield thy helmet and thy armour, yield thy gleaming sword and shield,
Hide thee from this deathful battle, matchless Karna rules the field!"

Sparkled Arjun's eye in anger with a red and livid flame,
And the tempest of his passion shook his more than mortal frame,

Heedless, on the sword-hilt Arjun placed his swift and trembling hand,
Heedless, with a warrior's instinct, drew the dark and glistening brand!

Sacred blood of king and elder would have stained his trenchant steel,
But the wise and noble Krishna strove the fatal feud to heal:

"Not before thy elder, Arjun, but in yonder purple field,
'Gainst thy rival and thy foeman use thy warlike sword and shield!

Render honour to thy elder, quench thy hasty, impious wrath,
Sin not 'gainst the holy *sastra*, leave not virtue's sacred path!

Bow before thy virtuous elder as before the gods in heaven,
Sheathe thy sword and quell thy passion, be thy hasty sin forgiven!"

Duteous Arjun silent listened and obeyed the mandate high,
Tears of manly sorrow trickled from his soft and altered eye,

Dear in joy and dear in suffering, calm his righteous elder stood,
Dear in Indra-prastha's mansions, dearer in the jungle wood!

Arjun sheathed his flashing sabre, joined his hands and hung his head,
Fixed his eye on good Yudhishthir and in humble accents said:

"Pardon, great and saintly monarch, vassal's disrespectful word,
Pardon, elder, if a younger heedless drew his sinful sword!

But thy hest to yield my weapon stung my soul to bitter strife,
Dearer is the bow *gandiva* unto Arjun than his life!

Pardon if the blood of anger mantled o'er this rugged brow,
Pardon if I drew my sabre 'gainst my duty and my vow!

For that hasty act repenting Arjun bows unto thy feet,
Grant me gentle king and elder, brother's love, forgiveness sweet!"

From Yudhishthir's altered eyelids gentle tears of sorrow start,
And he lifts his younger brother to his ever-loving heart:

"Arjun, I have wronged thee, brother, and no fault or sin is thine,
Hasty words of thoughtless anger 'scaped these sinful lips of mine!

Bitter was my shame and anguish when from Karna's car I fled,
Redder than my bleeding bosom warrior's fame and honour bled!

Hasty words I uttered, Arjun, by my pain and anguish driven,
Wipe them with a brother's kindness, be thy elder's sin forgiven!"

Stronger for his elder's blessing, Arjun mounts the battle-car,
Krishna drives the milk-white coursers to the thickening ranks of war!

Onward came the fiery Karna with his chiefs and arméd men,
Salya urged his flying coursers with the whip and loosened rein,

Often met and often parted, life-long rivals in their fame,
Not to part again, the heroes, each unto the other came,

Not to part until a chieftain by the other chief was slain,
Arjun dead or lifeless Karna pressed the Kuru-kshetra plain!

Long they strove, but neither archer could his gallant foeman beat,
Though like surging ocean billows did the angry warriors meet,

Arjun's arrows fell on Karna like the summer's angry flood,
Karna's shafts like hissing serpents drank the valiant Arjun's blood!

Fierce and quick from his *gandiva* angry accents Arjun woke,
Till the bow-string, strained and heated, was by sudden impulse broke,

"Hold," cried Arjun to his rival, "mind the honoured rules of war,
Warriors strike not helpless foemen thus disabled on the car,

Hold, brave Karna, until Arjun mends his over-strainéd bow,
Arjun then will crave for mercy nor from god nor mortal foe!"

Vain he spake, for wild with anger heedless Karna fiercely lowered,
Thick and fast on bowless Arjun countless arrows darkly showered,

Like the cobra, dark and hissing, Karna's gleaming arrows dart,
Strike the helpless archer Arjun on his broad and bleeding heart!

Furious like a wounded tiger quivering in the darksome wood,
With his mended warlike weapon now the angry Arjun stood,

Blazing with a mighty radiance like a flame in summer night,
Fierce he fell on archer Karna with his more than mortal might!

Little recked the dauntless Karna if his foe in anger rose,
Karna feared not face of mortal, dreaded not immortal foes,

Nor with all his wrath and valour Arjun conquered him in war,
Till within the soft earth sinking stuck the wheel of Karna's car!

Stood unmoved the tilted chariot, vainly wrathful Salya strove,
Urging still the struggling coursers Karna's heavy car to move,

Vainly too the gallant Karna leaped upon the humid soil,
Sought to lift the sunken axle with a hard unwonted toil,

"Hold," he cried to noble Arjun, "wage no false and impious war
On a foeman, helpless, carless,—thou upon thy lofty car."

Loudly laughed the helméd Arjun, answer nor rejoinder gave,
Unto Karna pleading virtue Krishna answered calm and grave:

"Didst thou seek the path of virtue, mighty Karna, archer bold,
When Sakuni robbed Yudhishthir of his empire and his gold?

Didst thou tread the path of honour on Yudhishthir's fatal fall,
Heaping insults on Draupadi in Hastina's council hall?

Didst thou then fulfil thy duty when, Yudhishthir's exile crost,
Krishna asked in right and justice for Yudhishthir's empire lost?

Didst thou fight a holy battle when with six marauders skilled,
Karna hunted Abhimanyu and the youthful hero killed?

Speak not then of rules of honour, blackened in your sins you die,
Death is come in shape of Arjun, Karna's fatal hour is nigh!"

Stung to fury and to madness, faint but frantic Karna fought,
Reckless, ruthless and relentless, valiant Arjun's life he sought!

Sent his last resistless arrow on his foeman's mighty chest,
Arjun felt a shock of thunder on his broad and mailéd breast!

Fainting fell the bleeding Arjun, darkness dimmed his manly eye,
Pale and breathless watched his warriors, anxious watched the gods in sky!

Then it passed, and helméd Arjun rose like newly lighted fire,
Abhimanyu's sad remembrance kindled fresh a father's ire!

And he drew his bow *gandiva*, aimed his dart with stifled breath,
Vengeance for his murdered hero winged the fatal dart of death!

Like the fiery bolt of lightning Arjun's lurid arrow sped,
Like the red and flaming meteor Karna fell among the dead!

III

Fall of Salya

Darkly closed the shades of midnight, Karna still and lifeless lay,
Ghast and pale o'er slaughtered thousands fell the morrow's sicklyray,

Bowman brave and proud preceptor, Kripa to Duryodhan said,
Tear bedimmed the warrior's eyelids and his manly bosom bled:

"Leaderless the Kuru forces, by a dire misfortune crost,
Like the moonless shades of midnight in their utter darkness lost!

Like a summer-driéd river, weary waste of arid sand,
Lost its pride of fresh'ning waters sweeping o'er the grateful land!

As a spark of fire consumeth summer's parched and sapless wood,
So thy lordless, lifeless forces shall be angry Arjun's food!

Bhima too will seek fulfilment of the dreadful vow he made,
Brave Satyaki wreak his vengeance for his sons untimely slayed!

Bid this battle cease, Duryodhan, pale and fitful is thy star,
Blood enough of friendly nations soaks this crimson field of war!

Bid them live,—the few survivors of a vast and countless host,
Let thy few remaining brothers live,—for many are the lost!

Kindly heart hath good Yudhishthir, still he seeks for rightful peace,
Render back his ancient kingdom, bid this war of kinsmen cease!"

कर्णवधः।

Fall of Karna

"Kripa," so Duryodhan answered, "in this sad and fatal strife,
Ever foremost of our warriors, ever careless of thy life,

Ever in the council chamber thou hast words of wisdom said,
Needless war and dire destruction by thy peaceful counsel stayed,

Every word that 'scapes thee, Kripa, is a word of truth and weight,
Nathless thy advice for concord, wise preceptor, comes too late!

Hope not that the good Yudhishthir will again our friendship own,
Cheated once by deep Sakuni of his kingdom and his throne,

Rugged Bhima will not palter, fatal is the vow he made,
Vengeful Arjun will not pardon gallant Abhimanyu dead!

Fair Draupadi doth her penance, so our ancient matrons say,
In our blood to wash her insult and her proud insulters slay,

Fair Subhadra morn and evening weeps her dear departed son,
Feeds Draupadi's deathless anger for the hero dead and gone,

Deeply in their bosoms rankle wrongs and insults we have given,
Blood alone can wash it, Kripa, such the cruel will of Heaven!

And the hour for peace is over, for our best sleep on the plain,
Brothers, kinsmen, friends, and elders slumber with the countless slain,

Shall Duryodhan like a recreant now avoid the deathful strife,
After all his bravest warriors have in war surrendered life?

Shall he, sending them to slaughter, now survive and learn to flee,
Shall he, ruler over monarchs, learn to bend the servile knee?

Proud Duryodhan sues no favour even with his dying breath,
Unsubdued and still unconquered, changeless even unto death!

Salya, valiant king of Madra, leads our arméd hosts to-day,
Or to perish o to conquer, gallant Kripa, lead the way!"

Meanwhile round the brave Yudhishthir calmly stood the Pandav force,
As the final day of battle now began its fatal course,

"Brothers, kinsmen, hero-warriors," so the good Yudhishthir said,
"Ye have done your share in battle, witness countless foemen dead,

Sad Yudhishthir is your eldest, let him end this fatal strife,
Slay the last of Kuru chieftains or surrender throne and life!

Bold Satyaki, ever faithful, with his arms protects my right,
Drupad's son with watchful valour guards my left with wonted might,

In the front doth Bhima battle, careful Arjun guards the rear,
I will lead the battle's centre which shall know nor flight nor fear!"

Truly on that fatal morning brave Yudhishthir kept his word,
Long and fiercely waged the combat with fair Madra's valiant lord,

Thick and fast the arrows whistled and the lances pointed well,
Crashing with the sound of thunder Salya's mighty standard fell!

Rescued by the son of Drona, Salya rushed again to war,
Slew the noble milk-white coursers of Yudhishthir's royal car,

And as springs the hungry lion on the spotted jungle-deer,
Salya rushed upon Yudhishthir reckless and unknown to fear!

Brave Yudhishthir marked him coming and he hurled his fatal dart,
Like the fatal curse of Brahman sank the weapon in his heart,

Blood suffused his eye and nostril, quivered still his feeble hand,
Like a cliff by thunder riven Salya fell and shook the land!

Ended was the fatal battle, for the *mlechcha* king was slain,
Pierced by angry Sahadeva false Sakuni pressed the plain,

All the brothers of Duryodhan tiger-waisted Bhima slew,
Proud Duryodhan pale and panting from the field of battle flew!

IV

Night of Slaughter

Far from battle's toil and slaughter, by a dark and limpid lake,
Sad and slow and faint Duryodhan did his humble shelter take,

But the valiant sons of Pandu, with the hunter's watchful care,
Thither tracked their fallen foeman like a wild beast in its lair!

' Gods be witness," said Duryodhan, flaming in his shame and wrath,
" Boy to manhood ever hating we have crossed each other's path,

Now we meet to part no longer, proud Duryodhan fights you all,
Perish he, or sons of Pandu, may this evening see your fall!"

Bhima answered: "For the insults long enduréd not forgiven,
Me alone you fight, Duryodhan, witness righteous gods in heaven!

Call to mind the dark destruction planned of old in fiendish ire,
In the halls of Varnavata to consume us in the fire!

Call to mind the scheme deceitful, deep Sakuni's dark device,
Cheating us of fame and empire by the trick of loaded dice!

Call to mind that coward insult and the outrage foul and keen,
Flung on Drupad's saintly daughter and our noble spotless queen!

Call to mind the stainless Bhishma for thy sins and folly slain,
Priest and proud perceptor Drona, Karna lifeless on the plain!

Perish in thy sins, Duryodhan, perish too thy hated name,
And thy dark life crime-polluted ends, Duryodhan, in thy shame!"

Like two bulls that fight in fury, blind with wounds and oozing blood,
Like two wild and warring tuskers shaking all the echoing wood,

Like the thunder-wielding INDRA, mighty YAMA dark and dread,
Dauntless Bhima and Duryodhan fiercely strove and fought and bled!

Sparks of fire shot from their maces and their faces ran with blood,
Neither won and neither yielded, matched in strength the rivals stood,

Then his vow remembered Bhima, and he raised his weapon high,
With a foul attack but fatal Bhima broke Duryodhan's thigh!

Through the sky a voice resounded as the great Duryodhan fell,
And the earth the voice re-echoed o'er her distant hill and dale,

Beasts and birds in consternation flew o'er land and azure sky,
Men below and heavenly *Siddhas* trembled at the fatal cry!

Darkness fell upon the battle, proud Duryodhan dying lay,
But the slaughter of the combat closed not with the closing day,

Ancient feud and hatred linger after battle's sweeping flood,
And the father's deathless anger courseth in the children's blood,

Drona slept and gallant Drupad, for their earthly task was done,
Vengeance fired the son of Drona 'gainst the royal Drupad's son!

Sable shadows of the midnight fell o'er battle's silent plain,
Faintly shone the fitful planets on the dying and the slain,

And the vengeful son of Drona, fired by omens dark and dread,
Stole into the tents of foemen with a soft and noiseless tread!

Dhrista-dyumna and Sikhandin, princes of Panchala's land,
Fell beneath the proud avenger Aswa-thaman's reeking hand,

Ay! where Drupad's sleeping grandsons, fair Draupadi's children lay,
Stole the cruel arm of vengeance, smothered them ere dawn of day!

Done the ghastly work of slaughter, Aswa-thaman bent his way
Where beside the limpid waters lone Duryodhan dying lay,

And Duryodhan blessed the hero with his feeble fleeting breath,
Joy of vengeance cheered his bosom as he died a happy death!

BOOK XI

SRADDHA

(Funeral Rites)

THE death of Duryodhan concludes the war, and it is followed by the lament of women and the funerals of the deceased warriors. The passages translated in this Book form Section x., portions of Sections xvi., xvii., and xxvi., and the whole of Section xxvii. of Book xi. of the original text.

I

Kuru Women visit the Battle-field

Spake the ancient Dhrita-rashtra, father of a hundred sons,
Sonless now and sorrow-stricken, dark his ebbing life-tide runs!

"Gods! fulfil my life's last wishes! Henchmen, yoke my royal car,
Dhrita-rashtra meets his princes in the silent field of war,

Speed unto the Queen Gandhari, to the dames of Kuru's house,
To each dear departed warrior wends his fair and faithful spouse!"

Queen Gandhari sorrow-laden with the ancient Pritha came,
And each weeping widowed princess and each wailing royal dame,

And they saw the hoary monarch, father of a perished race,
Fresh and loud awoke their sorrow, welling tears suffused their face,

Good Vidura ever gentle whispered comfort unto all,
Placed the dames within their chariots, left Hastina's palace hall!

Loud the wail of woe and sorrow rose from every Kuru house,
Children wept beside their mothers for each widowed royal spouse,

Veiléd dwellers of the palace, scarce the gods their face had seen,
Heedless now through mart and city wildly sped each widowed
queen,

From their royal brow and bosom gem and jewel cast aside,
Loose their robes and loose their tresses, quenched their haughty
queenly pride!

So when falls the antlered monarch, struck by woe and sudden fear
Issuing from their snowy mountains listless stray the dappled deer,

So upon the broad arena milk-white fillies brave the sun,
Wildly toss their flowing tresses and in sad disorder run!

Clinging to her weeping sister wept each dame in cureless pain,
For the lord, the son or father in the deathful battle slain,

Wept and smote her throbbing bosom and in bitter anguish wailed,
Till her senses reeled in sorrow, till her woman's reason failed!

Veiléd queens and bashful maidens, erst they shunned the public eye,
Blush nor shame suffused their faces as the city passed they by,

Gentle-bosomed, kindly hearted, erst they wiped each other's eye,
Now by common sorrow laden none for sister heaved a sigh!

With this troop of wailing women, deep in woe, disconsolate,
Slow the monarch of the Kurus passed Hastina's outer gate,

Men from stall and loom and anvil, men of every guild and trade,
Left the city with the monarch, through the open country strayed,

And a universal sorrow filled the air and answering sky,
As when ends the mortal's *Yuga* and the end of world is nigh!

धृतराष्ट्र विलापः।

Dhritarashtra's Lament.

II

Gandhari's Lament for the Slain

Stainless Queen and stainless woman, ever righteous ever good,
Stately in her mighty sorrow on the field Gandhari stood!

Strewn with skulls and clotted tresses, darkened by the stream of gore,
With the limbs of countless warriors was the red field covered o'er,

Elephants and steeds of battle, car-borne chiefs untimely slain,
Headless trunks and heads dissevered filled the red and ghastly plain!

And the long-drawn howl of jackals o'er the scene of carnage rings,
And the vulture and the raven flap their dark and loathsome wings,

Feasting on the blood of warriors foul *pisachas* fill the air,
Viewless forms of hungry *rakshas* limb from limb the corpses tear!

Through this scene of death and carnage was the ancient monarch led,
Kuru dames with faltering footsteps stepped amidst the countless dead,

And a piercing wail of anguish burst upon the echoing plain,
As they saw their sons or fathers, brothers, lords, amidst the slain,

As they saw the wolves of jungle feed upon the destined prey,
Darksome wanderers of the midnight prowling in the light of day!

Shriek of pain and wail of anguish o'er the ghastly field resound,
And their feeble footsteps falter and they sink upon the ground,

Sense and life desert the mourners as they faint in common grief,
Death-like swoon succeeding sorrow yields the sufferers short relief!

Then a mighty sigh of anguish from Gandhari's bosom broke,
Gazing on her anguished daughters unto Krishna thus she spoke:

"Mark my unconsoléd daughters, widowed queens of Kuru's house,
Wailing for their dear departed, like the osprey for her spouse!

How each cold and fading feature wakes in them a woman's love,
How amidst the lifeless warriors still with restless steps they rove,

Mothers hug their slaughtered children all unconscious in their sleep,
Widows bend upon their husbands and in ceaseless sorrow weep!

Mighty Bhishma, hath he fallen? quenched is archer Karna's pride?
Drupad monarch of Panchala sleeps by foeman Drona's side?

Shining mail and costly jewels, royal bangles strew the plain,
Golden garlands rich and burnished deck the chiefs untimely slain,

Lances hurled by stalwart fighters, clubs of mighty wrestlers killed,
Swords and bows of ample measure, quivers still with arrows filled!

Mark the unforgotten heroes, jungle prowlers 'mid them stray,
On their brow and mailéd bosoms heedless perch the birds of prey!

Mark the great unconquered heroes famed on earth from west to east,
Kankas perch upon their foreheads, hungry wolves upon them feast!

Mark the kings, on softest cushion scarce the needed rest they found,
How they lie in peaceful slumber on the hard and reddened ground!

Mark the youths who morn and evening listed to the minstrel's song,
In their ear the loathsome jackal doth his doleful wail prolong!

Mark the chieftains with their maces and the swords of trusty steel,
Still they grasp their tried weapons,—do they still the life-pulse feel?"

III

Gandhari's Lament for Duryodhan

Thus to Krishna, Queen Gandhari strove her woeful thoughts to tell,
When alas! her wandering vision on her son Duryodhan fell,

Sudden anguish smote her bosom and her senses seemed to stray,
Like a tree by tempest shaken senseless on the earth she lay!

Once again she waked in sorrow, once again she cast her eye
Where her son in blood empurpled slept beneath the open sky,

And she clasped her dear Duryodhan, held him close unto her breast,
Sobs convulsive shook her bosom as the lifeless form she prest,

And her tears like rains of summer fell and washed his noble head,
Decked with garlands still untarnished, graced with *nishkas* bright
and red!

"'Mother!' said my dear Duryodhan when he went unto the war,
'Wish me joy and wish me triumph as I mount the battle-car!'

'Son!' I said to dear Duryodhan, 'Heaven avert a cruel fate,
Yato dharma stato jayah! Triumph doth on Virtue wait!'

But he set his heart on battle, by his valour wiped his sins,
Now he dwells in realms celestial which the faithful warrior wins!

And I weep not for Duryodhan, like a prince he fought and fell,
But my sorrow-stricken husband, who can his misfortunes tell?

Ay! my son was brave and princely, all resistless in the war,
Now he sleeps the sleep of warriors, sunk in gloom his glorious star!

Ay! my son mid crownéd monarchs held the first and foremost way,
Now he rests upon the red earth, quenched his bright effulgent ray!

Ay! my son the best of heroes, he hath won the warrior's sky,
Kshatras nobly conquer, Krishna, when in war they nobly die!

Hark the loathsome cry of jackals, how the wolves their vigils keep,
Maidens rich in song and beauty erst were wont to watch his sleep!

Hark the foul and blood-beaked vultures flap their wings upon the dead,
Maidens waved their feathery *pankhas* round Duryodhan's royal bed!

Peerless bowman, mighty monarch! nations still his hests obeyed,
As a lion slays a tiger, Bhima hath Duryodhan slayed!

Thirteen years o'er Kuru's empire proud Duryodhan held his sway,
Ruled Hastina's ancient city where fair Ganga's waters stray!

I have seen his regal splendour with these ancieot eyes of mine,
Elephants and battle-chariots, steeds of war and herds of kine!

Kuru owns another master! And Duryodhan's day is fled!
And I live to be a witness! Krishna, O that I were dead!

Mark Duryodhan's noble widow, mother proud of Lakshman bold,
Queenly in her youth and beauty, like an altar of bright gold!

Torn from husband's sweet embraces, from her son's entwining arms,
Doomed to life-long woe and anguish in her youth and in her charms!

Rend my hard and stony bosom crushed beneath this cruel pain,
Should Gandhari live to witness noble son and grandson slain?

Mark again Duryodhan's widow, how she hugs his gory head,
How with gentle hands and tender softly holds him on his bed!

How from dear departed husband turns she to her dearer son,
And the tear-drops of the mother choke the widow's bitter groan!

Like the fibre of the lotus tender-golden is her frame,
O my lotus! O my daughter! woman's pride and Kuru's fame!

If the truth resides in *Vedas*, brave Duryodhan dwells above,
Wherefore linger we in sadness severed from his cherished love?

If the truth resides in *Sastra*, dwells in sky my hero son,
For Gandhari and her daughter now their earthly task is done!"

IV

Funeral Rite

Victor of a deathful battle, sad Yudhishthir viewed the plain,
Friends and kinsmen, kings and chieftains, countless troops untimely slain,

And he spake to wise Sudharman, pious priest of Kuru's race,
Unto Sanjay, unto Dhaumya, to Vidura full of grace,

Spake unto the brave Yuyutsu, Kuru's last surviving chief,
Spake to faithful Indrasena and to warriors sunk in grief:

"Pious rites are due to foemen and to friends and kinsmen slain,
None shall lack a fitting funeral, none shall perish on the plain."

Wise Vidura and his comrades sped on sacred duty bound,
Sandalwood and scented aloes, oil and *ghee* and perfumes found,

Silken robes of costly splendour, fabrics by the artist wove,
Dry wood from the thorny jungle, perfume from the scented grove,

Shattered cars and splintered lances, hewed and ready for the fire,
Piled and ranged in perfect order into many a funeral pyre.

Kings and princes, noble warriors, were in rank and order laid,
And with streams of melted butter were the rich libations made,

Blazed the fire with wondrous radiance by the rich libations fed,
Sanctifying and consuming mortal remnants of the dead.

Brave Duryodhan and his brothers, Salya of the mighty car,
Bhurisravas king of nations, Jayadratha famed in war,

Abhimanyu son of Arjun, Lakshman proud Duryodhan's son,
Somadatta and the Srinjays famed for deeds of valour done,

Matsya's monarch proud Virata, Drupad fair Panchala's king,
And his sons, Panchala's princes, whose great deeds the minstrels sing,

Cultured monarch of Kosala and Gandhara's wily lord,
Karna proud and peerless archer, matchless with his flaming sword,

Bhagadatta eastern monarch, all resistless in his car,
Ghatotkacha son of Bhima, Alambusha famed in war,

And a hundred other monarchs all received the pious rite,
Till the radiance of the fire-light chased the shadows of the night!

Pitri-medha, due to fathers, was performed with pious care,
Hymns and wails and lamentations mingled in the midnight air,

Sacred songs of *rik* and *saman* rose amidst the women's wail,
And the creatures of the wide earth heard the sound subdued and pale!

Smokeless and with radiant lustre shone each red and lighted pyre,
Like the planets of the bright sky throbbing with celestial fire!

Countless myriads, nameless, friendless, from each court and camp afar,
From the east and west collected, fell in Kuru-Kshetra's war,

Thousand fires for them were lighted, they received the pious rite,
Such was good Yudhishthir's mandate, such was wise Vidura's might,

All the dead were burned to ashes, and the sacred rite was o'er,
Dhrita-rashtra and Yudhishthir slowly walked to Ganga's shore.

V

Oblation to Karna

Sacred Ganga, ample-bosomed, sweeps along in regal pride,
Rolling down her limpid waters through high banks on either side,

Kuru dames and weeping widows thither in their anguish came
Due and holy rites to render to departed chiefs of fame.

Casting forth their jewelled girdles, gems and scarfs belaced with gold,
Gave oblations of the water to each hero true and bold,

Unto fathers, unto husbands, unto sons in battle slayed,
Offerings of the sacred water sorrowing wives and mothers made.

And so great the host of mourners wending to perform the rite,
That their footsteps made a pathway in the sad and sacred site,

And the shelving banks of Ganga peopled by the sorrowing train,
Wide-expanding, vast and sealike, formed a scene of woe and pain!

But a wave of keener sorrow swept o'er Pritha's heaving breast,
As unto her weeping children thus her secret she expressed:

"He, my sons, the peerless bowman, mighty in his battle-car,
He who bore the stamp of hero, slain by Arjun in the war,

He whom as the son of Radha, chariot-driver, ye have thought,
He who shone with SURYA's *lustre as his countless foes he fought,*

He who faced your stoutest warriors and in battle never failed,
He who led the Kuru forces and in danger never quailed,

He who knew no peer in prowess, owned in war no haughtier name,
He who yielded life, not honour, and by death hath conquered fame,

He, in truth who never faltered, never left his vow undone,
Offer unto him oblation! Karna was my eldest son!

Karna was your honoured elder, and the Sun inspired his birth,
Karna in his rings and armour Sun-like trod the spacious earth!"

Pritha spake, and terror-stricken Pandav brothers groaned in pain,
And they wept in woe and anguish for the brother they had slain!

Hissing forth his sigh of sorrow like a trodden, hissing snake
Sad Yudhishthir to his mother thus his inward anguish spake:

"Didst thou, mother, bear great Karna, fathomless like ocean dread,
Whose unfailing glistening arrows like its countless billows sped?

Didst thou bear that peerless archer, all-resistless in his car,
Sweeping with the roar of ocean through the shattered ranks of war?

Didst thou bear the mighty hero, mortal man of heavenly birth,
Crushing 'neath his arm of valour all his foemen on the earth?

Didst thou hide the birth and lineage of that chief of deathful ire,
As a man in folds of garments seeks to hide the flaming fire?

Arjun, wielder of *gandiva*, was for us no truer stay
Than was Karna for the Kurus in the battle's dread array!

Monarchs matched not Karna's glory nor his deeds of valour done,
Midst the mighty car-borne warriors mightiest warrior Karna shone!

Was he then our eldest brother we have in the battle slain,
And our nearest dearest elder fell upon the gory plain?

Not the death of Abhimanyu from the fair Subhadra torn,
Not the slaughter of the princes by the proud Draupadi borne,

Not the fall of Kuru warriors, nor Panchala's mighty host,
Like thy death afflicts my bosom, noble Karna! loved and lost!

Monarch's empire, victor's glory, all the treasures earth can yield,
Righteous bliss and heavenly gladness, harvest of the *swarga's* field,

All that wish can shape and utter, all that nourish hope and pride,
All were ours, O noble Karna! with thee by thy brothers' side,

And this carnage of the Kurus these sad eyes had never seen,
Peace had graced our blessed empire, happy would the earth have been!"

Long bewailed the sad Yudhishthir for his elder loved and dead,
And oblation of the water to the noble Karna made,

And the royal dames of Kuru viewed the sight with freshening pain,
Wept to see the good Yudhishthir offering to his brother slain,

And the widowed queen of Karna with the women of his house
Gave oblations to her hero, wept her loved and slaughtered spouse!

Done the rites to the departed, done oblations to the dead,
Slowly then the sad survivors on the river's margin spread,

Far along the shore and sandbank of the sacred sealike stream
Maid and matron laved their bodies 'neath the morning's holy beam,

And ablutions done, the Kurus slow and sad and cheerless part,
Wend their way to far Hastina with a void and vacant heart.

BOOK XII

ASWA-MEDHA

(Sacrifice of the Horse)

THE real Epic ends with the war and the funerals of the deceased warriors. Much of what follows in the original Sanscrit poem is either episodical, or comparatively recent interpolation. The great and venerable warrior Bhishma, still lying on his death-bed, discourses for the instruction of the newly crowned Yudhishthir on various subjects like the Duties of Kings, the Duties of the Four Castes, and the Four Stages of Life. He repeats the discourses of other saints, of Bhrigu and Bharadwaja, of Manu and Brihaspati, of Vyasa and Suka, of Yajnavalkya and Janaka, of Narada and Narayana. He explains *Sankhya* philosophy and *Yoga* philosophy, and lays down the laws of Marriage, the laws of Succession, the rules of Gifts, and the rules of Funeral Rites. He preaches the cult of Krishna, and narrates endless legends, tales, traditions, and myths about sages and saints, gods and mortal kings. All this is told in two Books containing about twenty-two thousand couplets, and forming nearly one-fourth of the entire Sanscrit Epic!

The reason of adding all this episodical and comparatively recent matter to the ancient Epic is not far to seek. The Epic became more popular with the nation at large than dry codes of law and philosophy, and generations of Brahmanical writers laboured therefore to insert in the Epic itself their rules of caste and moral conduct, their laws and philosophy. There is no more venerable character in the Epic than Bhishma, and these rules and laws have therefore been supposed to come from his lips on the solemn occasion of his death. As a storehouse of Hindu laws and traditions and moral rules these episodes are invaluable; but they form no part of the real Epic, they are not a portion of the leading story of the Epic and we pass them by.

Bhishma dies and is cremated; but the endless exposition of laws, legends, and moral rules is not yet over. Krishna himself takes up the task in a new Book, and, as he has done once before in the *Bhagavat-gita*, he now once more explains to Arjun in the *Anu-gita* the great truths about Soul and Emancipation, Creation and the Wheel of Life, True Knowledge and Rites and Penance. The adventures of the sage Utanka, whom Krishna meets, then take up a good many pages. All this forms no part of the real Epic, and we pass it by.

Yudhishthir has in the meantime been crowned king of the Kurus at Hastinapura, and a posthumous child of Abhimanyu is named Parikshit, and is destined to succeed to the throne of the Kurus. But Yudhishthir's mind is still troubled with the thoughts of the carnage of the war of which he considers himself guilty, and the great saint Vyasa advises the performance of the *aswa-medha*, or the Sacrifice of the Horse, for the expiation of the sin.

The Sacrifice of the Horse was an ancient Hindu custom practised by kings exercising suzerain powers over surrounding kings. A horse was let free, and was allowed to wander from place to place, accompanied by the king's guard. If any neighbouring king ventured to detain the animal, it was a signal for war. If no king ventured to restrain the wanderer, it was considered a tacit mark of submission to the owner of the animal. And when the horse returned from its peregrinations, it was sacrificed with great pomp and splendour at a feast to which all neighbouring kings were invited.

Yudhishthir allowed the sacrificial horse to wander at will, and Arjun accompanied it. Wherever the horse was stopped, Arjun fought and conquered, and thus proclaimed the supremacy of Yudhishthir over all neighbouring potentates. After various wars and adventures in various regions, Arjun at last returned victorious with the steed to Hastinapura, and the sacrifice commenced.

The description of the sacrifice is somewhat artificial, and concerns itself with rites and ceremonious details and gifts to Brahmans, and altogether bears unmistakable evidence of the interpolating hand of later priestly writers. Nevertheless we cannot exclude from this translation of the leading incidents of the Epic the last great and crowning act of Yudhishthir, now anointed monarch of Kuru-land.

The portion translated in this Book forms Sections lxxxv. and parts of Sections lxxxviii. and lxxxix. of Book xiv. of the original text.

I

The Gathering

Victor of a hundred battles, Arjun bent his homeward way,
Following still the sacred charger free to wander as it may,

Strolling minstrels to Yudhishthir spake of the returning steed,
Spake of Arjun wending homeward with the victor's crown of meed,

And they sang of Arjun's triumphs in Gandhara's distant vale,
On the banks of Brahmaputra and in Sindhu's rocky dale.

Twelfth day came of *magha's* bright moon, and auspicious was the star,
Nigher came the victor Arjun from his conquests near and far,

Good Yudhishthir called his brothers, faithful twins and Bhima true,
Spake to them in gentle accents, and his words were grave and few:

"Bhima! Now returneth Arjun with the steed from many-a fray,
So they tell me, noble brother, who have met him on the way,

And the time of *aswa-medha* day by day is drawing nigh,
Magha's full moon is approaching, and the cold month passeth by,

Let the Brahmans versed in Vedas choose the sacrificial site,
For the feast of many nations and performance of the rite."

Bhima heard of Arjun's coming,—hero with the curly hair,—
And to do Yudhishthir's mandate did with gladsome heart repair,

Brahmans versed in sacrifices, cunning architects of fame,
Builders of each various altar, with the son of Pritha came,

And upon a level greensward measured forth the sacred site,
Laid it out with halls and pathways for the sacrificial rite.

Mansions graced with gem and jewel round the bright arena shone,
Palaces of golden lustre glinted in the morning sun,

Gilt and blazoned with devices lofty columns stood around,
Graceful arches gold-surmounted spanned the consecrated ground,

Gay pavilions rose in beauty round the sacrificial site,
For the queens of crownéd monarchs wending to the holy rite,

Humbler dwellings rose for Brahmans, priests of learning and of fame,
Come to view Yudhishthir's *yajna* and to bless Yudhishthir's name.

Messengers with kindly greetings went to monarchs far-renowned,
Asked them to Hástina's city, and to grace the sacred ground,

And to please the great Yudhishthir came each king and chieftain bold,
With their slaves and dark-eyed damsels, arms and horses, gems and
gold,

Came and found a royal welcome in pavilions rich and high,
And the sealike voice of nations smote the echoing vault of sky!

With his greetings doth Yudhishthir, for each chief and king of men,
Cooling drinks and sumptuous viands, beds of regal pride ordain,

Stables filled with corn and barley and with milk and luscious cane
Greet the monarchs' warlike tuskers and the steeds with flowing mane.

Munis from their hermitages to the sacred *yajna* came,
Rishis from the grove and forest uttering BRAHMA's holy name,

Famed *Acharyas* versed in Vedas to the city held their way,
Brahmacharins with grass-girdle, chanting *rik* or *saman* lay,

Welcomed Kuru's pious monarch, saint and sage and man of grace,
And with gentle condescension showed each priest his fitting place.

Skilled mechanics, cunning artists, raised the structures for the rite,
And with every needful object graced the sacrificial site,

Every duty thus completed, joyful was Yudhishthir's mind,
And he blessed his faithful brothers with an elder's blessings kind.

II

The Feasting

Men in nations are assembled, hymns are sung by saint and sage,
And in learnéd disputations keen disputants oft engage,

And the concourse of the monarchs view the splendour of the rite,
Like the glorious sky of INDRA is the sacrificial site!

Bright festoons and flaming streamers o'er the golden arches hung,
Groups of men and gay-dressed women formed a bright and joyous
throng,

Jars of cool and sparkling waters, vessels rich with gold inlaid,
Costly cups and golden vases Kuru's wealth and pride displayed!

Sacrificial stakes of timber with their golden fastenings graced,
Consecrated by the *mantra* are in sumptuous order placed,

Countless creatures of the wide earth, fishes from the lake and flood,
Buffaloes and bulls from pasture, beasts of prey from jungle wood,

Birds and every egg-born creature, insects that from moisture spring,
Denizens of cave and mountain for the sacrifice they bring!

Noble chiefs and mighty monarchs gaze in wonder on the site,
Filled with every living object, corn and cattle for the rite,

Curd and cake and sweet confection are for feasting Brahmans spread,
And a hundred thousand people are with sumptuous viands fed!

With the accents of the rain-cloud drum and trumpet raise their voice,
Speak Yudhishthir's noble bounty, bid the sons of men rejoice,

Day by day the holy *yajna* grows in splendour and in joy,
Rice in hillocks feeds all comers, maid and matron, man and boy,

Lakes of curd and lakes of butter speak Yudhishthir's bounteous feast,
Nations of the Jambu-dwipa share it, greatest and the least!

For a hundred diverse races from each distant region came,
Ate of good Yudhishthir's bounty, blessed the good Yudhishthir's
name,

And a thousand proud attendants, gay with earrings, garland-graced,
Carried food unto the feeders and the sweet confections placed,

Viands fit for crownéd monarchs were unto the Brahmans given,
Drinks of rich and cooling fragrance like the nectar-drink of heaven!

III

Sacrifice of Animals

Victor of a hundred battles, Arjun came with conquering steed,
Vyasa, herald of the Vedas, bade the holy rite proceed:

"For the day is come, Yudhishthir, let the sacrifice be done,
And the priests repeat the *mantra* golden as the morning sun!

Threefold bounteous be thy presents, and a threefold merit gain,
For thy wealth of gold is ample, freely thy *dakshina* rain!

May the threefold rich performance purify the darkening stain,
Blood of warriors and of kinsmen slaughtered on the gory plain!

May the *yajna's* pure ablution wash thee of the cruel sin,
And the meed of sacrificers may the good Yudhishthir win!"

Return of the Sacrificial Horse.

Vyasa spake, and good Yudhishthir took the *diksha* of the rite,
And commenced the *aswa-medha* gladdening every living wight,

Round the altar's holy lustre moved the priests with sacred awe,
Swerved not from the rule of duty, failed not in the sacred law.

Done the rite of pure *pravargya* with the pious hymn and lay,
To the task of *abhishava* priests and Brahmans lead the way,

And the holy Soma-drinkers press the sacred Soma plant,
And perform the pure *savana* and the songs of *saman* chant.

Bounty waits on squalid hunger, gifts dispel the timid fear,
Gold revives the poor and lowly, mercy wipes the sufferer's tear,

Tender care relieves the stricken by the gracious king's command,
Charity with loving sweetness spreads her smile o'er all the land!

Day by day the *aswa-medha* doth with sacred rites proceed,
Day by day on royal bounty poor and grateful myriads feed,

And adept in six Vedangas, strict in vows and rich in lore,
Sage preceptors, holy teachers, grow in virtue ever more!

Six good stakes of *vilwa* timber, six of hard *khadira* wood,
Six of seasoned *sarvavarnin* on the place of *yajna* stood,

Two were made of *devadaru*, pine that on Himalay grows,
One was made of wood of *slesha* which the sacrificer knows,

Other stakes of golden lustre rich with skilful carvings done,
Draped in silk and gold-brocaded like the *ursa major* shone!

And the consecrated altar built and raised of bricks of gold,
Shone in splendour like the altar Daksha built in days of old,

Eighteen cubits square the structure, four deep lairs of brick in height,
With a spacious winged triangle like an eagle in its flight!

Beasts whose flesh is pure and wholesome, dwellers of the lake or sky,
Priests assigned each varied offering to each heavenly power on high,

Bulls of various breed and colour, steeds of mettle true and tried,
Other creatures, full three hundred, to the many stakes were tied.

Deva-rishis viewed the feasting, sweet *gandharvas* woke the song,
Apsaras like gleams of sunlight on the greensward tripped along,

Kinnaras and *kim-purushas* mingled in the holy rite,
Siddhas of austerest penance stood around the sacred site!

Vyasa's great and gifted pupils, who the Vedas have compiled,
Gazed upon the *aswa-medha,* on the wondrous *yajna* smiled,

From the bright ethereal mansions heavenly *rishi* Narad came,
Chetra-sena woke the music, singer of celestial fame,

Cheered by more than mortal music Brahmans to their task incline,
And Yudhishthir's fame and virtue with a brighter lustre shine!

IV

Sacrifice of the Horse

Birds and beasts thus immolated, dressed and cooked, provide the food,
Then before the sacred charger priests in rank and order stood,

And by rules of Veda guided slew the horse of noble breed,
Placed Draupadi, *Queen of yajna,* by the slain and lifeless steed,

Hymns and gifts and pure devotion sanctified the noble Queen,
Woman's worth and stainless virtue, woman's pride and wisdom keen!

Priests with holy contemplation cooked the horse with pious rite,
And the steam of welcome fragrance sanctified the sacred site,

Good Yudhishthir and his brothers, by the rules by *rishis* spoke,
Piously inhaled the fragrance and the sin-destroying smoke,

Severed limbs and sacred fragments of the courser duly dressed,
Priests upon the blazing altar as a pious offering placed,

And the ancient bard of Vedas, Vyasa raised his voice in song,
Blessed Yudhishthir, Kuru's monarch, and the many-nationed throng!

V

Gifts

Unto Brahmans gave Yudhishthir countless *nishkas* of bright gold,
Unto sage and saintly Vyasa all his realm and wealth untold,

But the bard and ancient *rishi* who the holy Vedas spake,
Rendered back the monarch's present, earthly gift he might not take!

"Thine is Kuru's ancient empire, rule the nations of the earth,
Gods have destined thee as monarch from the moment of thy birth,

Gold and wealth and rich *dakshina* let the priests and Brahmans hoard,
Be it thine to rule thy subjects as their father and their lord!"

Krishna too in gentle accents to the doubting monarch said:
"Vyasa speaketh word of wisdom and his mandate be obeyed!"

From the *rishi* good Yudhishthir then received the Kuru-land,
With a threefold gift of riches gladdened all the priestly band,

Pious priests and grateful nations to their distant regions went,
And his share of presents Vyasa to the ancient Pritha sent.

Fame and virtue Kuru's monarch by the *aswa-medha* wins,
And the rite of pure ablution cleanses all Yudhishthir's sins,

And he stands amid his brothers, brightly beaming, pure and high,
Even as INDRA stands surrounded by the dwellers of the sky,

And the concourse of the monarchs grace Yudhishthir's regal might,
As the radiant stars and planets grace the stillness of the night!

Gems and jewels in his bounty, gold and garments rich and rare,
Gave Yudhishthir to each monarch, slaves and damsels passing fair,

Loving gifts to dear relations gave the king of righteous fame,
And the grateful parting monarchs blessed Yudhishthir's hallowed name!

Last of all with many tear-drops Krishna mounts his lofty car,
Faithful still in joy or sorrow, faithful still in peace or war,

Arjun's comrade, Bhima's helper, good Yudhishthir's friend of yore,
Krishna leaves Hastina's mansions for the sea-girt Dwarka's shore!

CONCLUSION

THE real Epic ends with the war and with the funerals of the deceased warriors, as we have stated before, and Yudhishthir's Horse-Sacrifice is rather a crowning ornament than a part of the solid edifice. What follows the sacrifice is in no sense a part of the real Epic; it consists merely of concluding personal narratives of the heroes who have figured in the poem.

Dhrita-rashtra retires into a forest with his queen Gandhari, and Pritha, the mother of the Pandav brothers, accompanies them. In the solitude of the forest the old Dhrita-rashtra sees as in a vision the spirits of all the slain warriors, his sons and grandsons and kinsmen, clad and armed as they were in battle. The spirits disappear in the morning at the bidding of Vyasa who had called them up. At last Dhrita-rashtra and Gandhari and Pritha are burnt to death in a forest conflagration, death by fire being considered holy.

Krishna at Dwarka meets with strange and tragic adventures. The Vrishnis and the Andhakas become irreligious and addicted to drinking, and fall a prey to internal dissensions. Valadeva and Krishna die shortly after, and the city of the Yadavas is swallowed up by the ocean.

Then follow the two concluding Books of the Epic, the *Great Journey*, and the *Ascent to Heaven*, so beautifully rendered into English by Sir Edwin Arnold. On hearing of the death of their friend Krishna, the Pandav brothers place Prakshit, the grandson of Arjun, on the throne, and retire to the Himalayas. Draupadi drops down dead on the way, then Sahadeva, then Nakula, then Arjun, and then Bhima. Yudhishthir alone proceeds to heaven in person in a celestial car.

There Yudhishthir undergoes some trial, bathes in the celestial

Ganges, and rises with a celestial body. He then meets Krishna, now in his heavenly form, blazing in splendour and glory. He meets his brothers whom he had lost on earth, but who are now Immortals in the sky, clad in heavenly forms. INDRA himself appears before Yudhishthir, and introduces him to others who were dear to him on earth, and are dear to him in heaven. Thus speaks INDRA to Yudhishthir:

"This is She, the fair Immortal! Her no human mother bore,
Sprung from altar as Draupadi human shape for thee she wore,

By the Wielder of the trident she was waked to form and life,
Born in royal Drupad's mansion, righteous man, to be thy wife,

These are bright aërial beings, went for thee to lower earth,
Borne by Drupad's stainless daughter as thy children took their birth!

This is monarch Dhrita-rashtra who doth o'er *gandharvas* reign,
This is brave immortal Karna, erst on earth by Arjun slain,

Like the fire in ruddy splendour, for the Sun inspired his birth,
As the son of Chariot-driver he was known upon the earth!

'Midst the *Sadhyas* and the *Maruts*, 'midst immortals pure and bright,
Seek thy friends the faithful Vrishnis matchless in their warlike might,

Seek and find the brave Satyaki, him who served thy cause so well,
Seek the Bhojas and Andhakas who in Kuru-kshetra fell!

This is gallant Abhimanyu whom the fair Subhadra bore,
Still unconquered in the battle, slain by fraud in yonder shore,

Abhimanyu, son of Arjun, wielding Arjun's peerless might,
With the Lord of Night he ranges, beauteous as the Lord of Night!

This, Yudhishthir, is thy father! by thy mother joined in heaven,
Oft he comes into my mansions in his flowery chariot driven,

This is Bhishma, stainless warrior, by the *Vasus* is his place,
By the god of heavenly wisdom teacher Drona sits in grace!

These and other mighty warriors, in the earthly battle slain,
By their valour and their virtue walk the bright ethereal plain!

They have cast their mortal bodies, crossed the radiant gate of heaven,
For to win celestial mansions unto mortals it is given!

Let them strive by kindly action, gentle speech, endurance long,
Brighter life and holier future unto sons of men belong!"

TRANSLATOR'S EPILOGUE

ANCIENT India, like ancient Greece, boasts of two great Epics. One of them, the *Maha-bharata*, relates to a great war in which all the warlike races of Northern India took a share, and may therefore be compared to the Iliad. The other, the *Ramayana*, relates mainly to the adventures of its hero, banished from his country and wandering for long years in the wildernesses of Southern India, and may therefore be compared to the Odyssey. It is the first of these two Epics, the Iliad of Ancient India, which is the subject of the foregoing pages.

The great war which is the subject of this Epic is believed to have been fought in the thirteenth or fourteenth century before Christ. For generations and centuries after the war its main incidents must have been sung by bards and minstrels in the courts of Northern India. The war thus became the centre of a cycle of legends, songs, and poems in ancient India, even as Charlemagne and Arthur became the centres of legends in mediæval Europe. And then, probably under the direction of some enlightened king, the vast mass of legends and poetry, accumulated during centuries, was cast in a narrative form and formed the Epic of the Great Bharata nation, and therefore called the *Maha-bharata*. The real facts of the war had been obliterated by age, legendary heroes had become the principal actors, and, as is invariably the case in India, the thread of a high moral purpose, of the triumph of virtue and the subjugation of vice, was woven into the fabric of the great Epic.

We should have been thankful if this Epic, as it was thus originally put together some centuries before the Christian era, had been preserved to us. But this was not to be. The Epic became so popular that it went on growing with the growth of centuries. Every generation of poets had something to add; every distant nation in Northern India was anxious to interpolate some account of its deeds in the old record of the international war; every preacher of a new creed desired to have in the old Epic some sanction for the new truths he inculcated. Passages from legal and moral codes were incorporated in the work which appealed to the nation much more effectively than dry codes; and rules about the different castes and about the different stages of the human life were included for the same purpose. All the floating mass of tales, traditions, legends, and myths, for which ancient India was famous, found a shelter under the expanding wings of this wonderful Epic; and as Krishna-worship became the prevailing religion of India after the decay of Buddhism, the old Epic caught the complexion of the times, and Krishna-cult is its dominating religious idea in its present shape. It is thus that the work went on growing for a thousand years after it was first compiled and put together in the form of an Epic; until the crystal rill of the Epic itself was all but lost in an unending morass of religious and didactic episodes, legends, tales, and traditions.

When the mischief had been done, and the Epic had nearly assumed its present proportions, a few centuries after Christ according to the late Dr. Bühler, an attempt was made to prevent the further expansion of the work. The contents of the Epic were described in some prefatory verses, and the number of couplets in each Book was stated. The total number of couplets, according to this metrical preface, is about eighty-five thousand. But the limit so fixed has been exceeded in still later centuries; further additions and interpolations have been made; and the Epic as printed and published in Calcutta in this century contains over ninety thousand couplets, excluding the supplement about the race of Hari.

The modern reader will now understand the reason why this great Epic—the greatest work of imagination that Asia has produced—has never yet been put before the European reader in a readable form. A poem of ninety thousand couplets, about seven times the size of the Iliad and the Odyssey put together, is more than what the average reader can stand; and the heterogeneous nature of its contents does not add to the interest of the work. If the religious works of Hooker and Jeremy Taylor, the philosophy of Hobbes and Locke, the commentaries of Blackstone and the ballads of Percy, together with the tractarian writings of Newman, Keble, and Pusey, were all thrown into blank verse and incorporated with the *Paradise Lost*, the reader would scarcely be much to blame if he failed to appreciate that delectable compound. A complete translation of the *Maha-bharata* therefore into English verse is neither possible nor desirable, but portions of it have now and then been placed before English readers by distinguished writers. Dean Milman's graceful rendering of the story of Nala and Damayanti is still read and appreciated by a select circle of readers; and Sir Edwin Arnold's beautiful translation of the concluding books of the Epic is familiar to a larger circle of Englishmen. A complete translation of the Epic into English prose has also been published in India, and is useful to Sanscrit scholars for the purpose of reference.

But although the old Epic has thus been spoilt by unlimited expansion, yet nevertheless the leading incidents and characters of the real Epic are still discernible, uninjured by the mass of foreign substance in which they are embedded—even like those immortal marble figures which have been recovered from the ruins of an ancient world, and now beautify the museums of modern Europe. For years past I have thought that it was perhaps not impossible to exhume this buried Epic from the superincumbent mass of episodical matter, and to restore it to the modern world. For years past I have felt a longing to undertake this work, but the task was by no means an easy one. Leaving out all episodical matter, the leading narrative of the Epic forms about one-fourth of the work; and a complete translation even of this leading story would be unreadable, both from its length and its prolixness. On the other hand, to condense the story into shorter limits would be, not to make a translation, but virtually to write a new poem; and that was not what I desired to undertake, nor what I was competent to perform.

There seemed to me only one way out of this difficulty. The main incidents of Epic are narrated in the original work in passages which are neither diffuse nor unduly prolix, and which are interspersed in the leading narrative of the Epic, as that narrative itself is interspersed in the midst of more lengthy episodes. The more carefully I examined the arrangement, the more clearly it appeared to me that these main incidents of the Epic would bear a full and unabridged translation into English verse; and that these translations, linked together by short connecting notes, would virtually present the entire story of the Epic to the modern reader in a form and within limits which might be acceptable. It would be, no doubt, a condensed version of the original Epic, but the condensation would be effected, not by the translator telling a short story in his own language, but by linking together those passages of the original which describe the main and striking incidents, and thus telling the main story as told in the original work. The advantage of this arrangement is that, in the passages presented to the reader, it is the poet who speaks to him, not the translator. Though vast portions of the original are skipped over, those which are presented are the portions which narrate the main incidents of the Epic, and they describe those incidents as told by the poet himself.

This is the plan I have generally adopted in the present work. Except in the three books which describe the actual war (Books viii., ix., and x.), the other nine books of this translation are complete translations of selected passages of the original work. I have not attempted to condense these passages nor to expand them; I have endeavoured to put them before the English reader as they have been told by the poet in Sanscrit. Occasionally, but rarely, a few redundant couplets have been left out, or a long list of proper names or obscure allusions has been shortened; and in one place only, at the beginning of the Fifth Book, I have added twelve couplets of my own to explain the circumstances under which the story of Savitri is told. Generally, therefore, the translation may be accepted as an unabridged, though necessarily a free translation of the passages describing the main incidents of the Epic.

From this method I have been compelled to depart, much against my wish, in the three books describing the actual war. No translation of an Epic relating to a great war can be acceptable which does not narrate the main events of the war. The war of the *Maha-bharata* was a series of eighteen battles, fought on eighteen consecutive days, and I felt it necessary to present the reader with an account of each day's work. In order to do so, I have been compelled to condense, and not merely to translate selected passages. For the transactions of the war, unlike the other incidents of the Epic, have been narrated in the original with almost inconceivable prolixity and endless repetition; and the process of condensation in these three books has therefore been severe and thorough. But, nevertheless, even in these books I have endeavoured to preserve the character and the spirit of the original. Not only are the incidents narrated in the same order as in the original, but they are told in the style of the poet as far as possible. Even the similes and metaphors and figures of speech are all or mostly adopted from the original; the translator has not ventured either to adopt his own distinct style of narration, or to improve on the style of the original with his own decorations.

Such is the scheme I have adopted in presenting an Epic of ninety thousand Sanscrit couplets in about two thousand English couplets.

The excellent and deservedly popular prose translation of the Odyssey of Homer by Messrs. Butcher and Lang often led me to think that perhaps a prose translation of these selected passages from the *Maha-bharata* might be more acceptable to the modern reader. But a more serious consideration of the question dispelled that idea. Homer has an interest for the European reader which the *Maha-bharata* cannot lay claim to; as the father of European poetry he has a claim on the veneration of modern Europe which an Indian poet can never pretend to. To thousands of European readers Homer is familiar in the original, to hundreds of thousands he is known in various translations in various modern languages. What Homer actually wrote, a numerous class of students in Europe wish to know; and a literal prose translation therefore is welcome, after the great Epic has been so often translated in verse. The case is very different with the *Maha-bharata*, practically unknown to European readers. And the translators of Homer themselves gracefully acknowledge, "We have tried to transfer not all the truth about the poem, but the historical truth into English. In this process Homer must lose at least half his charm, his bright and equable speed, the musical current of that narrative, which, like the river of Egypt, flows from an undiscoverable source, and mirrors the temples and the palaces of unforgotten gods and kings. Without the music of verse, only a half truth about Homer can be told."

Another earnest worker of the present day, who is endeavouring to interpret to modern Englishmen the thoughts and sentiments and poetry of their Anglo-Saxon ancestors, has emphatically declared that "of all possible translations of poetry, a merely prose translation is the most inaccurate." "Prose," says Mr. Stopford Brooke, further on, "no more represents poetry than architecture does music. Translations of poetry are never much good, but at least they should always endeavour to have the musical movement of poetry, and to obey the laws of the verse they translate."

This appears to me to be a very sound maxim. And one of my greatest difficulties in the task I have undertaken has been to try and preserve something of the "musical movement" of the sonorous Sanscrit poetry in the English translation. Much of the Sanscrit Epic is written in the well-known *Sloka* metre of sixteen syllables in each line, and I endeavoured to choose some English metre which is familiar to the English ear, and which would reproduce to some extent the rhythm, the majesty, and the long and measured sweep of the Sanscrit verse. It was necessary to adopt such a metre in order to transfer something of the truth about the *Maha-bharata* into English, for without such reproduction or imitation of the musical movement of the original very much less than a half truth is told. My kind friend Mr. Edmund Russell, impelled by that enthusiasm for Indian poetry and Indian art which is a part of him, rendered me valuable help and assistance in this matter, and I gratefully acknowledge the benefit I have derived from his advice and suggestions. After considerable trouble and anxiety, and after rendering several books in different English metres, I felt convinced that the one finally adopted was a nearer approach to the Sanscrit *Sloka* than any other familiar English metre known to me.

I have recited a verse in this English metre and a *Sloka* in presence of listeners who have a better ear for music than myself, and they have marked the close resemblance. I quote a few lines from the Sanscrit showing varieties of the *Sloka* metre, and comparing them with the scheme of the English metre selected.

Esha Kuntisutah sriman | esha madhyama Pandavah
Esha putro Mahendrasya | Kurunam esha rakshita
—*Maha-bharata*, i. 5357.

Yet I doubt not through the ages | one increasing purpose runs
And the thoughts of men are widened | with the process of the suns
—*Locksley Hall.*

Malancha samupadaya | kanchanim samalamkritam
Avatirna tato rangam | Draupadi Bharatarshabha
—*Maha-bharata*, i. 6974.

Visions of the days departed | shadowy phantoms filled my brain;
Those who live in history only | seemed to walk the earth again
—*Belfry of Bruges.*

Asuryam iva suryena | nirvatam iva vayuna
Bhasitam hladitanchaiva | Krishnenedam sado hi nah
—*Maha-bharata*, ii. 1334.

Quaint old town of toil and traffic | quaint old town of art and song,
Memories haunt thy pointed gables, | like the rooks that round thee throng.
—*Nüremberg.*

Ha Pando ha maharaja | kvasi kim samupekshase

Putran vivasyatah sadhun | aribhir dyutanirjitan

—*Maha-bharata*, ii. 2610.

In her ear he whispers gaily, | If my heart by signs can tell,

Maiden I have watched thee daily, | And I think thou lov'st me well

—*Lord of Burleigh.*

It would be too much to assume that even with the help of this similarity in metres, I have been able to transfer into my English that sweep and majesty of verse which is the charm of Sanscrit, and which often sustains and elevates the simplest narration and the plainest ideas. Without the support of those sustaining wings, my poor narration must often plod through the dust; and I can only ask for the indulgence of the reader, which every translator of poetry from a foreign language can with reason ask, if the story as told in the translation is sometimes but a plain, simple, and homely narrative. For any artistic decoration I have neither the inclination nor the necessary qualification. The crisp and ornate style, the quaint expression, the chiselled word, the new-coined phrase, in which modern English poetry is rich, would scarcely suit the translation of an old Epic whose predominating characteristic is its simple and easy flow of narrative. Indeed, the *Maha-bharata* would lose that unadorned simplicity which is its first and foremost feature if the translator ventured to decorate it with the art of the modern day, even if he had been qualified to do so.

For if there is one characteristic feature which distinguishes the *Maha-bharata* (as well as the other Indian Epic, the *Ramayana*) from all later Sanscrit literature, it is the grand simplicity of its narrative, which contrasts with the artificial graces of later Sanscrit poetry. The poetry of Kalidasa, for instance, is ornate and beautiful, and almost scintillates with similes in every verse; the poetry of the *Maha-bharata* is plain and unpolished, and scarcely stoops to a simile or a figure of speech unless the simile comes naturally to the poet. The great deeds of godlike kings sometimes suggest to the poet the mighty deeds of gods; the rushing of warriors suggests the rushing of angry elephants in the echoing jungle; the flight of whistling arrows suggests the flight of sea-birds; the sound and movement of surging crowds suggest the heaving of billows; the erect attitude of a warrior suggests a tall cliff; the beauty of a maiden suggests the soft beauty of the blue lotús. When such comparisons come naturally to the poet, he aceepts them and notes them down, but he never seems to go in quest of them, he is never anxious to beautify and decorate. He seems to trust entirely to his grand narrative, to his heroic characters, to his stirring incidents, to hold millions of listeners in perpetual thrall. The majestic and sonorous Sanscrit metre is at his command, and even this he uses carelessly, and with frequent slips, known as *arsha* to later grammarians. The poet certainly seeks for no art to decorate his tale, he trusts to the lofty chronicle of bygone heroes to enchain the listening mankind.

And what heroes! In the delineation of character the *Maha-bharata* is far above anything which we find in later Sanscrit poetry. Indeed, with much that is fresh and sweet and lovely in later Sanscrit poetry, there is little or no portraiture of character. All heroes are cast much in the same heroic mould; all love-sick heroines suffer in silence and burn with fever, all fools are shrewd and impudent by turns, all knaves are heartless and cruel and suffer in the end. There is not much to distinguish between one warrior and another, between one tender woman and her sister. In the *Maha-bharata* we find just the reverse; each hero has a distinct individuality, a character of his own, clearly discernible from that of other heroes. No work of the imagination that could be named, *b*always excepting the Iliad, is so rich and so true as the *Maha harata* in the portraiture of the human character,—not in torment-and suffering as in Dante, not under overwhelming passions as in Shakespeare,—but human character in its calm dignity of strength and repose, like those immortal figures in marble which the ancients turned out, and which modern sculptors have vainly sought to reproduce. The old Kuru monarch Dhrita-rashtra, sightless and feeble, but majestic in his ancient grandeur; the noble grandsire Bhishma, "death's subduer" and unconquerable in war; the doughty Drona, venerable priest and vengeful warrior; and the proud and peerless archer Karna—have each a distinct character of his own which cannot be mistaken for a moment. The good and royal Yudhishthir, (I omit the final *a* in some long names which occur frequently), the "tiger-waisted" Bhima, and the "helmet-wearing" Arjun are the Agamemnon, the Ajax, and the Achilles of the Indian Epic. The proud and unyielding Duryodhan, and the fierce and fiery Duhsasan stand out foremost among the wrathful sons of the feeble old Kuru monarch. And Krishna possesses a character higher than that of Ulysses; unmatched in human wisdom, ever striving for righteousness and peace, he is thorough and unrelenting in war when war has begun. And the women of the Indian Epic possess characters as marked as those of the men. The stately and majestic queen Gandhari, the loving and doting mother Pritha, the proud and scornful Draupadi nursing her wrath till her wrongs are fearfully revenged, and the bright and brilliant and sunny Subhadra,—these are distinct images pencilled by the hand of a true master in the realm of creative imagination.

And if the characters of the *Maha-bharata* impress themselves on the reader, the incidents of the Epic are no less striking. Every scene on the shifting stage is a perfect and impressive picture. The tournament of the princes in which Arjun and Karna—the Achilles and Hector of the Indian Epic—first met and each marked the other for his foe; the gorgeous bridal of Draupadi; the equally gorgeous coronation of Yudhishthir and the death of the proud and boisterous Sisupala; the fatal game of dice and the scornful wrath of Draupadi against her insulters; the calm beauty of the forest life of the Pandavs; the cattle-lifting in Matsyaland in which the gallant Arjun threw off his disguise and stood forth as warrior and conqueror; and the Homeric speeches of the warriors in the council of war on the eve of the great contest,—each scene of this venerable old Epic impresses itself on the mind of the hushed and astonished reader. Then follows the war of eighteen days. The first few days are more or less uneventful, and have been condensed in this translation often into a few couplets; but the interest of the reader increases as he approaches the final battle and fall of the grand old fighter Bhishma. Then follows the stirring story of the death of Arjun's gallant boy, and Arjun's fierce revenge, and the death of the priest and warrior, doughty Drona. Last comes the crowning event of the Epic, the final contest between Arjun and Karna, the heroes of the Epic, and the war ends in a midnight slaughter and the death of the Duryodhan. The rest of the story is told in this translation in two books describing the funerals of the deceased warriors, and Yudhishthir's horse-sacrifice.

"The poems of Homer," says Mr. Gladstone, "differ from all other known poetry in this that they constitute in themselves an encyclopædia of life and knowledge; at a time when knowledge, indeed, such as lies beyond the bounds of actual experience, was extremely limited, and when life was singularly fresh, vivid, and expansive." This remark applies with even greater force to the *Maha-bharata;* it is an encyclopædia of the life and knowledge of Ancient India. And it discloses to us an ancient and forgotten world, a proud and noble civilisation which has passed away. Northern India was then parcelled among warlike races living side by side under their warlike kings, speaking the same language, performing the same religious rites and ceremonies, rejoicing in a common literature, rivalling each other in their schools of philosophy and learning as in the arts of peace and civilisation, and forming a confederation of Hindu nations unknown to, and unknowing the outside world. What this confederation of nations has done for the cause of human knowledge and human civilisation is a matter of history. Their inquiries into the hidden truths of religion, embalmed in the ancient *Upanishads*, have never been excelled within the last three thousand years. Their inquiries into philosophy, preserved in the *Sankhya* and the *Vedanta* systems, were the first systems of true philosophy which the world produced. And their great works of imagination, the *Maha-bharata* and the *Ramayana* will be placed without hesitation by the side of Homer by critics who survey the world's literatures from a lofty standpoint, and judge impartially of the wares turned out by the hand of man in all parts of the globe. It is scarcely necessary to add that the discoveries of the ancient Hindus in science, and specially in mathematics, are the heritage of the modern world; and that the lofty religion of Buddha, proclaimed in India five centuries before Christ, is now the religion of a third of the human race.

For the rest, the people of modern India know how to appreciate their ancient heritage. It is not an exaggeration to state that the two hundred millions of Hindus of the present day cherish in their hearts the story of their ancient Epics. The Hindu scarcely lives, man or woman, high or low, educated or ignorant, whose earliest recollections do not cling round the story and the characters of the great Epics. The almost illiterate oil-manufacturer or confectioner of Bengal spells out some modern translation of the *Maha-bharata* to while away his leisure hour. The tall and stalwart peasantry of the North-West know of the five Pandav brothers, and of their friend the righteous Krishna. The people of Bombay and Madras cherish with equal ardour the story of the righteous war. And even the traditions and tales interspersed in the Epic, and which spoil the work as an Epic, have themselves a charm and an attraction; and the morals inculcated in these tales sink into the hearts of a naturally religious people, and form the basis of their moral education. Mothers in India know no better theme for imparting wisdom and instruction to their daughters, and elderly men know no richer storehouse for narrating tales to children, than these stories preserved in the Epics. No work in Europe, not Homer in Greece or Virgil in Italy, not Shakespeare or Milton in English-speaking lands, is the *national* property of the nations to the same extent as the Epics of India are of the Hindus. No single work except the Bible has such influence in affording moral instruction in Christian lands as the *Maha-bharata* and the *Ramayana* in India. They have been the cherished heritage of the Hindus for three thousand years; they are to the present day interwoven with the thoughts and beliefs and moral ideas of a nation numbering two hundred millions.

ROMESH DUTT.

UNIVERSITY COLLEGE, LONDON,
13th August 1898.

GLOSSARY OF SANSCRIT WORDS

Abhishava, a religious rite.
Abhisheka, sacred ablution.
Acharya, preceptor.
Ajya, a form of sacrificial offering.
Apramatta, without pride or passion.
Apsaras, celestial nymphs.
Arghya, offering due to an honoured guest.
Arya, noble.
Asram, hermitage.
Asura, Titans, enemies of gods.
Aswamedha, sacrifice of the horse.

Baidurya, lapiz-lazuli.
Brahmacharin, one who has taken vows and lives an austere life.

Chandan, sandalwood, the paste of which is used for fragrance and coolness.
Chowri or **Chamari**, the Himalayan yak, whose bushy tail is used as a fan.

Dakshina, gifts made at sacrifices.
Dasaputra, son of a slave.
Deva, gods.
Devadaru (*lit.* heavenly tree), the Indian pine.
Deva-kanva, celestial maid.
Deva-rishi, celestial saint.
Dharma-raja, monarch by reason of piety and virtue.
Diksha, initiation into a sacred rite.

Gandharva, a class of aerial beings; celestial singers.
Gandiva, Arjun's bow.
Ghee or **Ghrita**, clarified butter.
Guru, preceptor.

Homa, a sacrificial rite or offering.
Howda, the seat on an elephant.

Ida, a form of sacrificial offering.

Kanka, a bird of prey.
Khadira, an Indian tree.
Kimpurusha, a class of imaginary beings.
Kinnara, a class of imaginary beings with the face of a horse.
Kokil, an Indian bird answering to the English cuckoo, and prized for its sweet note.

Magha, a winter month.
Mahut or **Mahamatra**, elephant driver.
Mantra, hymn or incantation.
Mlechcha, outer barbarian. All who were not Hindus were designated by this name.
Muni, saint, anchorite.

Naga, dweller of the snake-world; also a tribe in Eastern India.
Nishada, an aboriginal race.
Nishka, gold pieces of specified weight, used as money and also as ornament.

PANKHA (from Sanscrit *paksha*, wing), a fan.
PISHACHA, ghost or goblin.
PITRI-MEDHA, sacrifice and offering due to departed ancestors.
PRAVARGYA, a religious rite.
PURANA, a class of religious works.
PURUSHA, the soul.

RAJASUVA, imperial sacrifice.
RAKSHA or RAKSHASA, monster or goblin.
RIK, hymn recited at sacrifice.
RISHI, saint; a holy man retired from the world and devoting himself to pious rites and contemplation.

SAMADHI, austere religious practice.
SAMAN, hymn chanted at sacrifice.
SAMI, an Indian tree.
SANKHA, sounding conch-shell.
SARVAVARNIN, an Indian tree.
SASTRA, scriptures and religious works.
SAVANA, a religious rite.
SAVITRI, a hymn; also the goddess of the hymn.
SIDDHA, holy celestial beings.
SLESHA, an Indian tree.
SUPARNA, celestial bird.
SWARGA, heaven.
SWASTI, a word uttered to dispel evil.
SWAYAMVARA, a form of bridal, the bride selecting her husband from among suitors.

TIRTHA, holy rites at the crossing of rivers.
TRIRATRA, a three nights' penance and fast.

VEDA, the oldest and holiest scriptures of the Hindus.
VIJAYA, Karna's bow.
VINA, the lyre.

YAJNA, sacrifice.
YATO DHARMA STATO JAYAH, where there is virtue there is victory.
YUGA, the period of the world's existence.